DR. OETKER

GERMAN BAKING TODAY

THE ORIGINAL

DR. OETKER

GERMAN BAKING TODAY

THE ORIGINAL

Ceres-Verlag
Rudolf-August Oetker KG
Bielefeld

Copyright:	© 1987 Ceres-Verlag Rudolf-August Oetker KG, Bielefeld
Editor:	Gisela Knutzen
Recipe development and text:	Test kitchen, Dr. August Oetker, Bielefeld Annette Elges, Bielefeld
Cover photography:	Thomas Diercks, Hamburg
Inside photography:	Thomas Diercks, Hamburg Brigitte Wegner, Bielefeld
Reproductions:	Pörtner & Saletzki, Bielefeld
Typesetting:	Hanke & Pettke, Bielefeld
Printing:	Kaufmann, Lahr

ISBN 3-7670-0365-1

BAKING IS FUN – Those of you who enjoy baking cakes, gateaux and biscuits will find this book invaluable.

In Germany it has been used successfully by many generations to help with their baking for special occasions as well as the daily tea table.

This new and completely revised edition has kept the concise structure of the original.

The sections are split up by types of pastry, and the text and illustrations make the step by step instructions easy to follow, guaranteeing perfect results for both professional cooks and absolute beginners.

Popular traditional recipes have been updated and new wholefood recipes have been added, as well as new recipes for confectionery.

The essential information section is richly illustrated and tells you all you ever wanted, or needed, to know about baking.

Just follow the instructions in the recipes and you will see that BAKING IS FUN!

Table of Contents

Essential Information Page 10

Table of Contents

Stirred cake mixtures

Sponge cake mixtures

Kneaded pastry

Yeast doughs and pastries

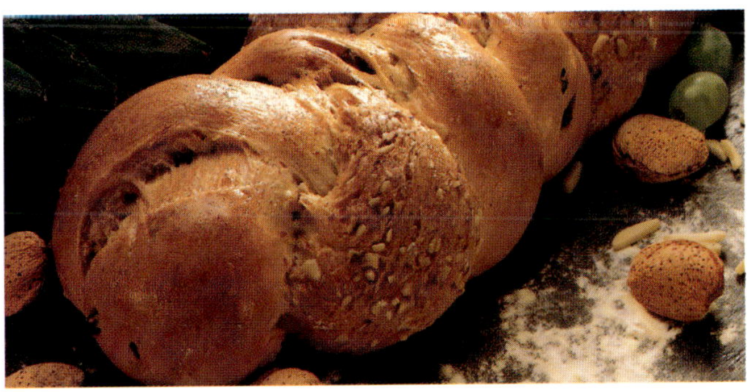

Table of Contents

Table of Contents

Baking utensils

Practical baking utensils

Suitable and practical utensils are a must for both the professional baker and the beginner. The quality of bakeware and utensils influences the quality of the finished product.

Bowls (1) are needed in a variety of sizes.

- Sturdy plastic bowls with a rubber ring on the base to prevent slipping are best for making pastry, mixing cakes, and whipping cream or egg white. If other bowls are used, it is advisable to stand them on a damp cloth.
- Stainless steel bowls conduct heat well. This makes them ideal for use over a water bath, e.g. for melting or softening glazes.

Measuring and weighing equipment is of the greatest importance to ensure that recipes can be followed exactly, e.g. a good set of kitchen scales (2), preferably with an add and weigh dial, and a clearly marked measuring jug (3). A large variety of equipment is available in the shops.

Mixing spoons (4) (preferably with a hole) for stirring ingredients together.

Pastry wheel (5) for cutting rolled out pastry, giving it an attractively bevelled edge.

Kitchen scissors, e.g. for cutting pastry.

Metal spatula (6) a large, wide but blunt knife or similar, with which rolled-out pastry can be loosened from the pastry board if it sticks. Also useful for smoothing creams on to cakes or lifting small cakes or biscuits.

Hand whisks (7) in a variety of sizes, e.g. for whipping cream, beating eggs or creams and for folding ingredients into delicate mixtures.

Pastry brush (8) for greasing baking pans or brushing egg, milk, etc. on to pastry or cakes.

Timer to help you stick to the baking times in the recipe.

Spatula to remove cake mixture from the mixing bowl and for smoothing the mixture in the baking pan.

Almond/nut grinder with a number of inserts.

Cake rack to allow cakes and pastries to cool off. If cakes and pastries are left to cool in the pan or on a plate, they will be soggy underneath.

Graters, e.g. for lemon peel or chocolate.

Piping bag (9) with a variety of nozzles, e.g. for decorating cakes or piping pastry.

Pastry cutters (10) for cookies and Christmas biscuits.

Cake board, stainless steel or sturdy plastic, e.g. for moving cakes or lifting off cake layers.

Sieves for flour, cornflour, cocoa or baking powder. The one-hand baking sieve is recommended for small quantities.

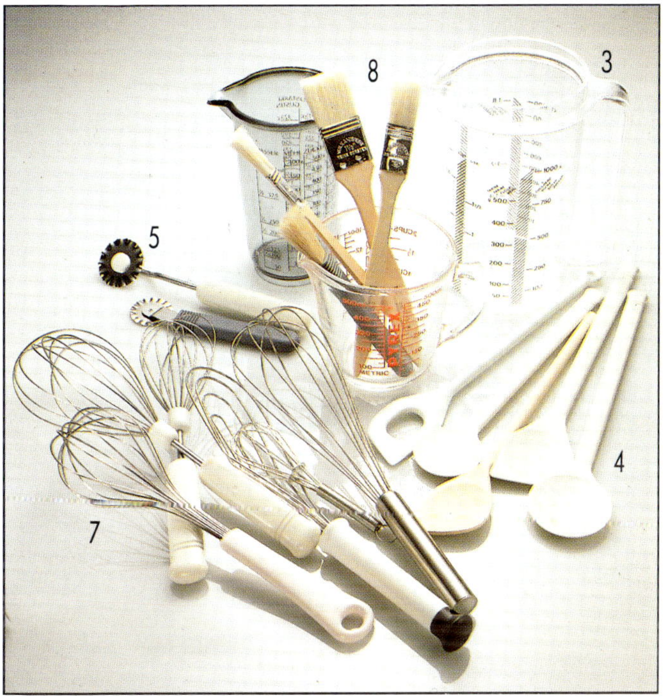

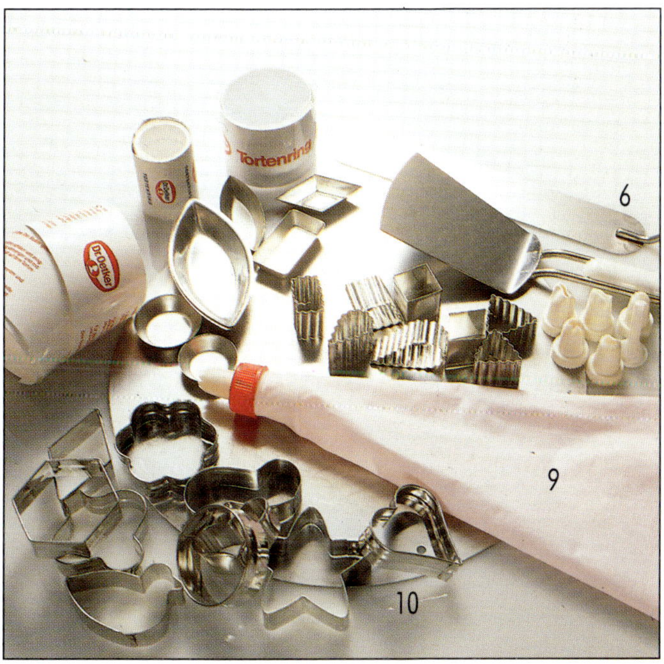

Rolling pin made from wood or plastic. Helps you roll pastry out evenly and can be used for crushing hard ingredients (e.g. almond brittle).

Cake divider, makes it easy to divide a cake into equal slices.

Baking pans

Baking pans

The material from which baking pans are made has a major influence of the successful baking of various types of cake and pastry mixtures. When buying baking pans it is also important to take account of your type of oven.

A. The Material

Tin bakeware

Tin bakeware is ideal for use where direct heat is applied, e.g. gas oven. It is less suitable for use in electric ovens.
Before using tin bakeware for the first time, it should be seasoned. To do this, heat the empty baking pans in the oven for 30 minutes at baking temperature.
Tin bakeware should always be placed on the wire shelf, on the low position, in the oven. This ensures that the heat from underneath takes effect first, ensuring even browning.

Aluminium bakeware

Aluminium is a metal with good heat conducting properties, and is corrosion resistant.
Aluminium bakeware is suitable for use in all types of oven.

Black lacquered bakeware

Black bakeware absorbs a lot of heat and transfers it immediately to the contents. It is ideal for use in electric and hot air convection ovens. If used in gas ovens, a lower temperature setting should be chosen in conjunction with a higher shelf position.

Non-stick bakeware

Today's non-stick linings have proved ideal in all types of oven. The thicker walls of non-stick bakeware are better able to store the heat, thus saving energy. Cakes come out of non-stick baking pans easily, even if the pans were not evenly greased. Non-stick bakeware always gives good results.
There is a renewed trend towards heavy bakeware. This has a professional image because of
a) its non-stick coating and
b) the good, heavy quality of the material – up to 0,8 mm steel sheeting.
These qualities guarantee durability and a long life, as well as very good heat conductivity and excellent baking results.

Ceramic bakeware

Ceramic bakeware stores heat before transferring it to the contents of the mould. This type of bakeware can be used in all types of oven.
Attractive ceramic bakeware is not only good to bake in, it also makes attractive decoration for the kitchen walls.

B. Different types of baking pan

The traditional cake pans are angel cake, loaf, flan and springform pans. The latter have exchangeable flat and tube bases. Every kitchen should contain at least 3 or 4 different cake pans.

At least one baking sheet is supplied with every new oven. Baking sheets are suitable for baking a number of types of cakes and pastry, e.g. fruit cake, Swiss rolls, baked shapes, small pastries and cookies.

There are a lot of other traditional baking pans such as clover leaf, heart, rosette, star or log shapes. Other types such as tree, butterfly, shell or animal shapes are not essential but provide variety and give traditional cakes a new look.

The fact that many of these baking pans are available in mini-sizes is a bonus for small households.

A number of shapes are available for small cakes and pastries such as mini flans, tartlets, etc. Disposable paper cup cake cases are also available.

A note on cleaning cake pans: it is always best to wash baking pans directly after use, when they are still warm. Washing is especially easy in the case of pans with a non-stick coating.

Baked-on pastry should never be removed by scraping with a sharp implement or by scouring. Simply steep the pan in warm water for a few minutes and then wash normally and dry well.

Types of energy: Gas/electricity/convection heat

The development of cooker ovens

Gas ovens were widely used in years gone by, but were difficult to regulate with the constantly burning jets. Nowadays 78 out of 100 households have electric ovens.

Ovens with conventional heating

In this form of oven, the heat is produced at the top and bottom. Generally speaking, these ovens take a little longer to preheat and they operate at higher temperatures than multi-choice ovens.

Ovens with hot air systems

An intensive stream of hot air, produced by a ventilator motor positioned inside a circular heater, surrounds the food and cooks it. The air is heated and continually circulated around the oven. This system permits food to be cooked simultaneously on all of the oven shelves. This type of oven operates at lower temperatures than conventional ones, i.e. 20 – 30° C lower.

Temperature settings

Gas	Electricity	Hot Air	Use for:
	50°	50°	Proving yeast dough
	75°	75°	Keeping food warm, warming crockery
1	100°-125°	100°-125°	Drying biscuits slowly (macaroons)
2	175°	160°	Sterilizing (preserving)
2	175°-190°	160°-170°	High cakes (madeira cake)
3	200°	160°-180°	Medium cakes (yeastcake)
3-4	210°-225°	160°-180°	Flat cakes
5-6	225°-250°	180°-190°	Gratinating

Multiple choice ovens

The latest ovens offer multiple choice. This means that the user can set the oven to conventional cooking or hot air convection. AEG cookers and ovens also offer the:

- 4-shelf hot-air system, for baking large quantities of cakes and cookies, and for thawing and preserving,
- conventional top and bottom heat for baking bread and rolls, as well as other options such as,
- infratherm grills for gratinating,
- surface grills.

AEG VITRATHERM ovens

offer even greater improvements in their heating systems. These ovens are available built-in or free-standing and have their top and bottom heating elements fitted behind transparent ceramic glass panels. Advantages:

- easier to clean because no heating element gets in the way
- larger oven area available
- less danger of burns because the heating element cannot be touched directly, and, last but not least
- a larger grill surface for better grilling results.

Oven with ceramic glass ceiling, AEG VITRATHERM. Top heat and grill are tucked safely away behind glass. A new type of oven heating with a number of benefits (see left).

Built-in AEG oven with integrated microwave function, types EX 64.1 LV and EX 640.1 G. Ideal ovens to shorten cooking times (see below).

Ovens with integrated microwave function.

These ovens also represent a new development. The microwave function can be switched on to accompany one of the multi-choice functions. This gives the following benefits:

– cooking is speeded up, mostly at lower power, and food still browns.

Microwaves have only limited value for baking, e.g. for cakes with a low proportion of flour, such as yeastcake, cheesecake, nut cake, etc.

Weights/Measures/Baking Temperatures

Weights and Measures

Weighing and measuring ingredients exactly is a precondition for successful baking.

Dry ingredients such as sugar, flour, dried fruit etc. should be weighed on kitchen scales; teaspoons or tablespoons can be used for small quantities. Special measuring jugs are available for liquids, see p. 00; teaspoons or tablespoons can also be used for smaller quantities.

10 g flour =	1 level tbs
25 g flour =	1 heaped tbs
2 g cornflour =	1 level tsp
10 g cornflour =	1 lightly heaped tbs
15 g cornflour =	1 heaped tbs
3 g baking powder =	1 level tsp
10 g sugar/icing sugar =	1 heaped tsp
15 g sugar/icing sugar =	1 level tbs
20 g sugar/icing sugar =	1 lightly heaped tbs
5 g cocoa =	1 level tbs
10 g breadcrumbs =	1 level tbs
12 g semolina =	1 level tbs
125 ml (1/8 l) milk =	8 tbs
15 g fat =	1 level tbs
5 g salt =	1 level tsp

Baking temperatures

Electricity, gas, convection heat

The use of the correct temperature setting for baking is just as important as following the recipe instructions carefully.

This means that a cook not only needs to know how to prepare the various types of pastry, but must also be familiar with her or his oven.

The baking times given in the individual recipes can be longer or shorter depending on the oven, the type of energy it uses and the condition of the ingredients themselves. For this reason it is advisable to check the cake or pastry frequently towards the end of the baking time to find out whether it is baked through. To do this, push a wooden skewer into the centre of the cake. If it comes out clean, the cake is ready.

All mixtures that are to be baked in baking pans should be placed on the wire shelf in the oven and not on a baking sheet or the oven floor, otherwise the base of the cakes will be too dark or, in the case of the baking sheet, not properly baked, because not enough heat gets through.

Electric and gas ovens

1. Ovens with top and bottom heat (radiation heat)
These ovens can be set to a given temperature by means of a selector. In gas ovens the temperatures range between settings 0 and 8 and in electric ovens between 0 and 250. Before cakes etc. are put into the oven it should be preheated to the required temperature (10-15 minutes).
This applies especially to electric ovens. Gas and hot air convection ovens heat up very quickly and need little or no preheating. When the oven has reached the set temperature, the indicator light will go out and the oven is ready to use. High and medium high baking pans are generally placed on the wire shelf in the lowest shelf position, low pans on the wire shelf in the middle position. Flat cakes, biscuits, stollen, choux buns and meringues are usually baked in the centre of the oven, although biscuits can be baked on a higher shelf. However, it is always important to follow the oven manufacturer's instructions. As already mentioned, a number of items can be placed in a gas oven that has not been preheated, especially cakes in high and medium high baking pans. Pastries and small loaf shapes are better baked in a preheated oven as this prevents them from losing their shape.

2. Hot air convection ovens
In this type of oven, the air is circulated by means of a ventilator and flows evenly around the oven contents. This means that it is possible to bake on 4 levels at once. This highly efficient circulation of air allows you to bake at lower temperatures than usual, without preheating the oven. Individual ovens function differently within their given temperature ranges, and it is always essential to follow the manufacturer's instructions exactly.
Generally speaking, it is safe to assume that the temperature in a hot air convection oven can be set 10 – 15% lower than in a conventional oven. The more intense heat browns food more quickly.
IMPORTANT. If baking items with long cooking times (more than 30 minutes) in an electric oven, i.e. a conventional oven with top and bottom heat or a hot air convection oven, remember that the oven can be switched off about 5 minutes before the end of the cooking time. Baking will continue in the heat retained in the oven.

3. Multiple choice ovens
These are ovens with conventional top and bottom heat as well as hot air convection. The cook decides which function will be used.

4. Ovens with integrated microwave
These ovens are available in the following combinations:
- Top and bottom heat with microwave
- Hot air convection with microwave
- Top and bottom heat and hot air convection with microwave.

The heating and microwave functions can be used separately or together. The manufacturer's instructions must be followed closely.

Baking ingredients

Important baking ingredients

Aniseed
Very aromatic seeds with a sweet fragrance. Once ground the aroma is soon lost. Buy in small quantities just before it is needed.

Maple syrup
Juice of the sugar maple; mostly produced in Canada and the US state of Vermont. Used for baking (especially wholegrain baking), jams and ice-cream preparations.

Baking powder
A raising agent made from sodium bicarbonate, an acid carrier and a separating agent. Carbon dioxide is produced during baking, and is released from the pastry.

Bakers yeast
A biological raising agent. Available fresh and dried.

Rice paper
Super thin, round or square, edible base, e.g. for macaroons or gingerbread. Made from flour or cornflour with no raising agent.

Bitter almonds
Fruit of the bitter almond tree. Bitter taste with hydrocyanic acid content. Only the tiniest amounts should be used for flavouring.

Peanuts
Peeled nuts of the groundnut family. Use in the same way as other nuts and almonds.

Muscovado sugar
Yellow to dark brown sugar made from the juice of sugar cane. Used for ginger or honey cake.

Gelatine
A gelling agent used in baking, e.g. for cream, fresh cream or jelly fillings.

Crushed sugar candy
Crushed brown sugar candy is very aromatic and is used for baking all sorts of gingerbreads. It can also be used for decorating biscuits in the same way as coarse crystallized sugar.

Crystallized sugar
Coarse crystallized sugar is used for decorating biscuits.

Hartshorn salt
A chemical raising agent made from ammonium carbonate or ammonium and carbonic acid. At temperatures in excess of 60° C, it splits up into ammonia, water and, particularly, carbon dioxide, which lightens the pastry. Especially suitable for flat gingerbread biscuits (high cakes can retain residual ammonia). It decomposes on contact with air and must be kept in well sealed containers.

Honey
A natural product produced by bees from flower nectar. Various flavours. Liquid to solid consistence. Frequently used in wholegrain baking and Christmas biscuits.

Ginger
Spice made from the root of the ginger plant. Available fresh, ground, dried, preserved in syrup or candied. Strong, spicy slightly hot flavour.

Cardamom
Dried seed capsules of annual coriander. Available whole or

ground. Slightly hot, spicy taste. Mainly used in Christmas biscuits.

Potato starch
Edible starch produced from potatoes.

Desiccated coconut
Grated flesh of the coconut. Limited shelf life as only available unsulfurated.

Coriander
Dried fruit of the coriander shrub. Sweet, aromatic aroma. Available whole, crushed or ground. Very popular for spicy biscuits.

Currants
Unsulfurated, dried, red to blackish violet, seedless berries of the grape family. Their flavour and aroma are stronger than those of raisins.

Brittle
Made from caramelized sugar and at least 20% nuts and almonds.

Chocolate glaze
Chocolate glaze in various flavours. Used for coating biscuits, adding to cake mixtures and pastries, and for fillings and creams.

Almonds
Fruit of the almond tree. Available peeled, unpeeled, whole, chopped, ground, flaked or split.

Almond paste Produced mainly from sweet almonds and sugar. Suitable for fillings, pastries, sweets and decoration.

Poppy seeds
Oily seeds of the poppy plant. Used for fillings or as a pastry ingredient (whole or ground).

Nutmeg
Nutmeg flower, mace. The red seed covering that surrounds the nut. Mild aroma, delicate flavour. Nutmeg, fruit of the evergreen nutmeg tree. Strong, spicy flavour. Should be used sparingly. Both spices are available whole or ground.

Cloves
The dark brown flower buds of the clove tree, harvested just before they open. Available dried and whole or ground. Potent aroma with a strong, slightly hot flavour. Use very sparingly.

Nougat
Concentrated soft mixture made from peeled nut kernels, sugar and cocoa products. Should be stirred until soft or melted, before it is used as a cake ingredient. Cake and gateau fillings, decorations.

Candied orange peel
Normally available chopped or as half skins. Used in cakes or for decoration.

Baking ingredients

Pine nuts
Oily seeds from pine trees that grow in Mediterranean countries. Similar in flavour to almonds. Used for cakes, fillings and decoration.

Pistachios
Pale green coloured nuts of the pistachio tree. Normally available shelled. Used for fillings, cakes and decoration.

Potash
Chemical raising agent made from potassium carbonate. White, odourless, slightly soapy-tasting powder. Lightens pastry only in conjunction with acid. Used for honey pastry.

Rosewater
By-product (condensate) of rose oil extraction. Used to flavour pastries and marzipan.

Raisins (Sultanas)
Air-dried, pale or dark coloured, seedless berries from a variety of vines. Available sulfurated or unsulfurated, e.g. for cakes, fillings or decoration.

Saffron
The dried stamens of a Mediterranean crocus. Gives strong colour and has a slightly bitter taste. Use sparingly.

Cream stiffener
Powder and special starch product that is whipped into cream to keep it stiff and prevent separation.

Sesame seeds
Seeds of the tropical sesame plant. Used for baking, flavouring vegetables and salads.

Soy flour
Soy flour is produced from soy beans which are mainly grown in East Asia. It gives an individual flavour to pastry etc.

Starch
Cornflour or potato starch used as a thickener for puddings, sauces and creams. Can be mixed with flour for baking.

Star Anise
Seed covering of this spice tree which grows in Southern China. Similar flavour to aniseed. Popular for Christmas baking, bread, desserts and sauces.

Vanilla
The fermented seed pod of a climbing orchid. The inside of the pod is scraped out or the whole pod can be used chopped up and ground.

Cinnamon
Dried inner bark of the cinnamon tree. For baking, the spicy, mild Ceylon cinnamon is preferable to the spicy and strong Kassia cinnamon from China.

Sugar
Sugar is manufactured from sugar cane or sugar beet. Recipes may call for refined sugar, granulated sugar, brown sugar or icing sugar.

The most important thing to remember, whatever the recipe, is that all ingredients should be as fresh as possible. Inferior ingredients or ingredients that have been stored for too long can ruin your baking.

Vanilla flavoured sugar
Available in small packets. This is sugar that has been flavoured with vanilla or artificial vanilla flavouring.

Candied lemon peel
Usually available diced but can also be bought in half skins. Used in pastry cakes and for decoration.

Cereals

Types of cereal

All grains, i.e. wheat, rye, oats, barley, sorghum, etc. contain valuable nutrients that form an important part of our basic diet. Of those grains shown on these pages, wheat has become the most important type of grain used for baking in central Europe. This is because products milled from wheat have the best baking characteristics.

Wheat is used for cake and pastry making. It contains a large proportion of gluten as well as potassium, phosphorus, magnesium and B-complex vitamins.

Rye is used mainly for making bread. It contains high quality protein, potassium, phosphorus, magnesium and calcium.

Barley contains gluten and is only suitable for baking when used in conjunction with other grains. It contains a high proportion of protein, potassium, phosphorus, magnesium and vitamin B.

Oats are available as groats, flour and flakes. Oats are rich in protein, vitamins and minerals.

A cereal grain is made up of 3 main parts:

1. **The germ**
   The germ is made up of grains of starch and protein. The cell walls are made of cellulose. The outer layer is called the aleurone layer and contains high proportions of protein, minerals and vitamins.
2. **The outer layers = the fruit and seed husks**
   The husks surround the germ and the sprout. They are made up of a number of layers rich in minerals and fibre.
3. **The sprout**
   In addition to important vitamins and trace elements, the sprout is rich in vegetable protein and high quality vegetable fats.

Buckwheat is very good for baking although it is advisable to mix it with wheat flour. Buckwheat is not a cereal but a knotgrass. It is rich in minerals, vitamins and lecithin.

Greencorn is spelt that is harvested when only half ripe. After harvesting it is carefully dried. It is used in the same way as flour for baking. Greencorn contains calcium and phosphorus.

Spelt is a form of wheat. It is very rich in gluten, calcium and phosphorus and is excellent for baking.

Sorghum is used in wholefood baking for crisp biscuits. It is rich in minerals, especially phosphorus, magnesium, iron and B-complex vitamins.

Maize. Due to its lack of gluten, maize is only of limited value for baking. It is frequently mixed with other cereals. Maize is rich in fat and this gives it a short shelf life.

Types of flour

The different types of flour

Turning grain into flour is a long and complicated process. Milling the cleaned and stored grain can take up to 20 separate steps.
First the grain is crushed on rollers. It is then sieved to separate the bran and the sprouts. Continued sieving grades the endosperm by size. Further milling results in semolina (hard or soft semolina, depending on the type of wheat). The penultimate milling stage results in a fine type of flour known as "dunst". This is followed by the last stage of milling which results in the most popular type of plain flour for baking. In Germany this is called type 405.
In Germany a large number of different types of flour are available, and generally speaking the higher the type number, the stronger the flour, i.e. the higher the wholegrain content. Flours with higher type numbers (e.g. type 1050) contain more of the nutrients contained in the outer layers of the grain and are correspondingly darker in colour.
In your home country you will find flour graded from fine (cakes) to strong (bread etc.). The self-raising flour that is available in the UK and USA contains baking powder. This is not available in Germany, so the recipes include baking powder, which must be added to flour to make cakes and pastries rise. The most popular types of flour available in Germany are shown opposite.

Fine white flour type 405 (1)

This is the finest and whitest flour, and is the most popular type for baking. Flour type 405 has excellent baking properties, because it contains a high proportion of the endosperm protein. This protein swells when the wet dough or mixture is baked, giving the finished item firmness and stability and a finely grained structure.

Dunst (2)

is a very fine type of flour that makes the preparation of heavy doughs much easier. Yeast pastries rise better and strudel pastry is lighter when dunst is used.

Strong plain flour type 1050 (3).

This contains a particularly high proportion of the outer layers of the wheat grain and is therefore rich in valuable minerals, vitamins and fibre. Its excellent baking properties make it ideal for bread and flavourful pastry.

Wholegrain wheat flour (4)

is milled from strong, high quality wheat grains complete with bran. The high proportion of bran gives the flour its pleasant brown colour and full flavour and makes it an important addition to a healthy diet.

Soft wheat semolina (5)

is very fine, contains no husks and is milled from soft wheat.

Hard wheat semolina (6)

is coarser, hard and strongly flavoured. It is milled exclusively from high quality, golden yellow durum wheat. Hard wheat semolina is excellent for baked dishes, dumplings and pasta.

Rye flour type 997 (7)

This dark, strong flour is full of valuable minerals. It contains plenty of fibre to aid digestion and contains higher quality proteins than most other types of cereal. This combined with its full flavour makes it an ideal flour for bread baking.

Wholegrain rye flour type 1800 (8)

This is flour milled from whole rye. It can be finely or coarsely milled.

Baking fats

Fats for baking

Margarine, butter and vegetable oils are the fats most used for baking. Apart from most sponges, no cake mixture or pastry is prepared without fat. Fat is very important for the consistency of pastry etc. and gives it its short or spongy texture.

Margarine

This is an emulsion of approx. 80% fat and 20% water. Margarine contains approx. 1% of other ingredients such as vitamins and lecithin (important as a stabilizing agent for the emulsion).

Margarine is mainly made from vegetable raw ingredients such as corn, sunflower or soy oil. It is a spreadable fat mixture.

Depending on their application, margarines are made to varying recipes and from a variety of raw ingredients. Vegetable margarines, for example, contain only vegetable fats, and diet margarines contain a higher proportion of polyunsaturated fatty acids.

Depending on their composition, margarines can also vary in consistency. Slab margarines spread less easily than those supplied in containers.
Margarine retains its spreadability even in the refrigerator and can therefore be used for baking without first having to bring it to room temperature.

Sanella is a favourite baking margarine in Germany. It softens quickly and combines well with the other ingredients. Cakes and pastry made with Sanella are fine grained and have an even consistency.

Butter

This is an emulsion of at least 82% milk fat and no more than 16% water. As opposed to margarine, butter becomes very hard in the refrigerator and must be brought to room temperature before it can be used for baking.

Vegetable oil

Vegetable oil is frequently used for quark and oil doughs and also for yeast doughs. It is produced mainly from soy beans, sunflower seed or olives. It is advisable to use a neutral tasting oil to avoid adding unwanted flavour to cakes and pastries.

White fats

The so-called white fats (in Germany, Biskin and Palmin for example) are made from pure vegetable fat. One advantage of these fats is their high heat stability. White fats have a high smoking point and are therefore eminently suitable for frying, braising and deep frying, as these forms of cooking demand high temperatures for browning and crisping. Neutral tasting white coconut fat is ideal for preparing cake glazes.

Mixing pastry in a food processor

A food processor takes all the drudgery out of baking and cooking. It stands firmly on the work surface and leaves your hands free to operate it and add ingredients, etc. Large quantities of cake batter can be mixed, bread dough kneaded and cream whipped, all effortlessly.
Our recipes are all intended for use with a hand mixer, and we have not included instructions for manual preparation.
Today's food processors are ideal for large and small households. They are compact, versatile and safe to use. A wide range of attachments will deal with most kitchen chores, e.g. milling grain, chopping and grinding nuts, squeezing citrus fruits, mixing drinks, grating and chopping vegetables, preparing fruit and vegetable juice, slicing and grating potatoes, and much more.

How to use the BOSCH MUM 4400 table top mixer and food processor

The Bosch MUM 4400 table-top mixer and food processor shown opposite has a wide range of attachments for many applications. The 4 speed settings permit mixing to start slowly and then be speeded up when all the ingredients have been worked in.

Method for various types of cake batter, pastry and dough:

Stirred cake batter, using the beater
Mix and sieve the flour with the baking powder, then put it into the mixing bowl with all the other ingredients (except dried fruit and chocolate), ensuring that the fat is soft enough to spread.
Switch the appliance on to "1" for about 1 – 2 minutes, then switch to "3" and allow to run for about 1 minute. Switch off the appliance, scrape the batter from the sides of the bowl to the centre.
Switch on to "3" and allow to run for a further 1 – 2 minutes. Any fruit that is to be added should be quickly folded in last on setting "1".

Kneaded dough, using the kneading attachment
Mix and sieve the flour with the baking powder and put it into the mixing bowl with all the other ingredients, making sure the fat is soft enough to spread. Run the mixer for about 1 – 2 minute on "1"; run for a further 1 – 2 minutes until the ingredients are well combined.

Quark and oil dough, using the kneading attachment
Mix and sieve the flour with the baking powder and put it into the mixing bowl with all the other ingredients. Run the mixer for about 1 minute on "2". Do not mix for too long, as the dough could become sticky. Dust a pastry board with flour and shape the dough into a roll on it.

Sponge cake batter, using the beater
Put eggs and hot water into the mixing bowl, add the sugar and vanilla sugar, and beat for 4 minutes on "4". Switch the appliance back to "2", slowly sieve in the flour mixed with baking powder (takes about 1 – 2 minute). If done too quickly the batter will be lumpy and if done too slowly the finished cake will be heavy.

Yeast dough, using the kneading attachment
Sieve the flour (no more than 500 g at a time) into the mixing bowl and mix it carefully with the dried yeast (exception: for doughs containing a lot of ingredients, e.g. fruit loaf, the yeast must first be mixed with warm water or milk). Add all the other ingredients to the flour. Run the appliance for 1 – 2 minute on "1", then switch to "2" and run for 3 – 4 minutes.

Choux pastry, using the beater
When you get to the hot pastry "dumpling" stage, put the pastry into the mixing bowl and slowly work in the eggs. Work each egg in separately on setting "2-3", until you have a smooth dough. Keep switching off the mixer and testing the consistency of the dough. No more egg need be added when the choux is very shiny and drops leaving long strands. Work in the baking powder last.

Food processors

How to use the AEG Finesse plus compact food processor

The uncomplicated construction of this kitchen appliance makes it very easy to use. The Finesse plus will mix and knead any type of dough or batter.
Its special feature is the plastic blade with which it quickly and gently mixes ingredients into a light dough or batter. The infinitely adjustable electronic switch ensures that the appliance always works with the right number of rpm.

Methods for preparing the various types of pastry and batter

Stirred cake batter, using plastic blade (method A)
Mix and sieve the flour with the baking powder, and put it into the mixing bowl with all the other ingredients (including dried fruit), ensuring that the fat is soft enough to spread. Switch the appliance on to "3" for a moment, then switch to "12" and allow to run for about 1½ minutes. Switch off the appliance; scrape the batter from the sides of the bowl to the centre.

(Method B)
Put the sugar, soft fat, eggs and spices into the mixing bowl and mix for about 1 minute on "12". Switch off the appliance, scrape the batter from the sides of the bowl to the centre. Now add the sieved flour mixed with the baking powder and mix for 1 minute on "12". Finally fold in any fruit quickly on "3".

Kneaded dough, using plastic blade
Sieve and mix the flour with baking powder, and put it into the mixing bowl with all the other ingredients, making sure the fat is soft enough to spread. Run the mixer for a moment on "3" then knead on "12" until the ingredients are well combined in a smooth dough. Shape the dough into a roll on the work surface and use as directed in the recipe.

Sponge cake batter, using the beater
Put eggs and hot water into the mixing bowl and beat for about 1 minute on "9". Add the sugar and vanilla sugar and beat for 2 minutes more. Add the flour mixed with baking powder and cornflour in 3 portions on "3". Use the mixture as directed in the recipe.

Yeast dough, using the plastic blade
Sieve the flour (no more than 500 g at a time) into the mixing bowl and mix it carefully with the dried yeast (exception: for doughs containing a lot of ingredients, e.g. fruit loaf, the yeast must first be mixed with warm water or milk). Add all the other ingredients to the flour (including fruit). Run the appliance for a moment on "3", then switch to "12" and run for 1 – 2 minutes until the dough is smooth and comes away from the sides of the bowl. Leave to rise.

Quark and oil dough, using the plastic blade
Mix and sieve the flour with the baking powder, and put it into the mixing bowl with all the other ingredients. Run the mixer for a moment on "3" then mix for a further ½ – 1 minute on "12". Do not mix for too long as the dough could become sticky. Use as directed in the recipe.

Choux pastry, using the plastic blade
When you get to the hot pastry "dumpling" stage, put the pastry into the mixing bowl and slowly work in the eggs one at a time on "6" until you have a smooth dough. Keep switching off the mixer and testing the consistency of the dough. No more egg need be added when the choux is very shiny and leaves long strands when dropped. Work in the baking powder last. Use as directed in the recipe.

IMPULS
MAX.
AEG
FINESSE PLUS
electronic
MAX.
6 - MAX.
3 - 9
1 - 4
4 - MAX.

Baking hints

General baking hints

If a recipe calls for almonds, they should first be dropped into boiling water, then boiled up for a moment, drained and refreshed with cold water. Peel and use as directed.

Bake flan cases blind (i.e. without the filling) to keep them crisp and stop them becoming soggy with juicy fillings. To do this, line a flan case with pastry and prick the base of the pastry several times to allow any air to escape. Make sure the base stays flat.

The bottom of the flan can also be covered with lentils, split peas or dried beans to keep it flat and stop the sides from slipping down.

Baking pans should be greased thoroughly with soft butter or margarine. Angel cake pans or loaf tins can also be sprinkled inside with breadcrumbs, desiccated coconut, ground nuts or almonds.

When individual flan cases have been greased, stand them close to each other and cover loosely with a sheet of pastry. Lightly press the pastry into the cases, roll over the top with the rolling pin, pressing on the edges. Cut out the shapes with a knife.

To split a flan horizontally, first make a cut where the split is to be. Take a piece of thread around the flan and into the cut. Cross the ends of the thread and pull firmly. The flan will be split cleanly in two.

Before chocolate is grated, refrigerate it thoroughly. Cold chocolate is easier to grate. Melt glaze over a water bath.

Delicate rounds of pastry can be easily transferred to the baking sheet if they are rolled over a floured rolling pin and rolled off on to the baking sheet.

If you want to reduce sponge fingers or rusks to crumbs, put them into a freezer bag, seal and then crush with a rolling pin.

When mixing cake batter, put a damp cloth under the mixing bowl so that it cannot slip away and pull the paper on to the

Butter cream will not curdle if the butter and the custard are at the same temperature, i.e. the butter must not be straight out of the fridge, and the custard must have been allowed to cool.

If you only have one baking sheet but need to make a large number of biscuits, cut a number of pieces of greaseproof paper to the size of your baking sheet. Place the cut out biscuits on the greaseproof paper

baking sheet over the flat edge. This stops the biscuits from sliding about and lets you bake them one sheet after another. (See photo below)

Hints for wholemeal baking

In many recipes it is not possible to swap plain white flour weight for weight for wholemeal flour. The gluten content will make the pastry swell and become heavy.
Work kneaded doughs and pastries before allowing them to rest, e.g. line a baking pan, shape pastries or cut out shapes. They are easier to work before the gluten has had a chance to swell.
When using wholemeal flour, it is advisable to take extra baking powder or raising agent. The high gluten content makes the pastry heavier and less able to rise.
Stick to baking times otherwise your finished product could be dry and crumbly.
When using wholemeal flour, sugar should be replaced by honey or maple syrup.
Sugar cannot be swapped weight for weight against honey or maple syrup as this would make the pastry too soft, i.e. the consistency would be wrong.

Shaping pastry

Yeast pastry turnovers

Roll out the pastry into rounds about 10 cm in diameter. Place the filling on the centre of the round. Brush the edges of the pastry with a little beaten egg. Fold the round in half to enclose the filling. Press the edges of the pastry together with the end of a spoon.

Windmills

Roll puff pastry out thinly and cut into 10 x 10 cm squares. Make cuts about 5 cm long from the corners to the centre. Place a stewed apricot half in the centre of each square. Fold one corner of each section to the centre of the apricot.

Twists

Roll out yeast pastry thinly and cut into rectangles. Make a cut down the middle of each rectangle and pull the outer edge through the middle.

Plaited loaves

Divide yeast dough into three pieces and shape into long rolls. Form a plait with the three rolls.

Puff pastry envelopes

Roll puff pastry out thinly and cut into 10 x 10 cm squares. Place a little filling in the centre of each square. Fold each corner into the centre of the filling.

Crescents

Roll out puff pastry to a sheet 72 x 14 cm and cut into triangles (the longest side of the triangle should be about 12 cm long). Brush the edges of the pastry with a little condensed milk. Place a little filling near the wide edge and roll the pastry up into crescent shapes.

Cake and pastry decoration

Colourfully decorated cakes and biscuits are attractive and appetizing. Schwartau offers a whole range of decorative and chocolate products, candied fruit, almonds, nuts, glazes and marzipan. However, their products are not just to entice the eye; they cab be used as ingredients, coatings and fillings, and are important ingredients in a large variety of cakes and pastries. The illustrations on these pages show some examples, and the many cakes and biscuits on the following pages use them in the recipes.

The chocolate tartlets are delicious when filled with fruit and whipped cream and decorated with chocolate leaves.
Simple biscuits move into the luxury range when decorated with chocolate drops, chocolate tree bark, coffee beans and meringue stars.
Essential ingredients such as almonds, nuts, pistachio nuts, brittle, candied fruit, marzipan, nut nougat, etc. can also double as unusual decorations on Christmas cookies (see photo on left).

For children's parties decorate biscuits and cake with sugar flowers, rainbow sugar, coloured sugar writing, hundreds and thousands, etc. Children love lots of colour. The many colourful flowers and beads are stuck on to the cold cakes and biscuits with melted chocolate glaze, egg-white or icing (photo above).

TIP:
For parties, dip the rims of glasses into water and then into rainbow sugar for decoration.

What can go wrong?

Things that can go wrong and how to prevent them

When deep frying fat starts to foam.
If fat is not hot enough it can start to foam when food is put into it. This can tear delicate pastries apart. It is therefore important to check whether the fat is at the right temperature before dropping any pastry into it. If the fat starts to bubble when the stem of a wooden spoon is dipped into it, the temperature is right.

When baking powder turns pink.
This happens when baking powder is stored alongside baking spices such as vanilla sugar or cinnamon. It is better to store baking powder separately in a tightly sealed tin in a cool place. The discoloration is not detrimental to the efficiency of the baking powder.

When yeast refuses to rise.
Dr. Oetker dried yeast is preserved in a special process. Yeast needs warmth. The temperature in the kitchen should be at least 22° C. Lukewarm water and milk should be at body temperature (37° C).

When gelatine goes lumpy.
If gelatine starts to get lumpy or stringy, this means that the liquid in which it is being dissolved is too cold. Ensure that all ingredients are at room temperature, i.e. not under 15°C.

When kneaded pastry is too soft.
If pastry with a high fat content has turned out to be too soft during kneading, it can be refrigerated to stiffen it up. If, however, it is soft because it contains too much liquid (eggs, milk or water), extra flour should be kneaded into it.

When all the raisins have dropped to the bottom of the cake.
When this happens it means that the mixture was too soft. Cake mixture should have a heavy dropping consistency.

When sponges sink.
It is important to stick to the specified times when preparing sponge cake batter in a food processor. Batters which have been beaten for too long will rise beautifully at first but, because they are too light, will then collapse. Check whether sponge cake is baked by laying the flat of your hand on the surface of the cake. It should feel soft and a little like cotton wool before it may be removed from the oven.

When cake crumbles on cutting.
When cutting cake do not press down the blade of the knife, use it in a sawing motion. A serrated knife blade (breadknife) is recommended.

When some parts of your stirred cake are still sticky.
This is normally because too much milk has been used in the batter. The batter should have a heavy dropping consistency. Never add so much milk that the batter is semi-liquid.

When kneaded pastry won't roll out.
One reason for this can be the use of spreading or soft margarine. Normal, firm baking margarine should be used.

When your stirred batter cake has holes in it.
Irregular air holes result when the batter has been beaten for too long after the flour/baking powder mixture was added. This can be avoided by folding the mixture in quickly, 2 – 3 tbs at a time.

When the fruit flan is soggy.
Juice from the fruit can soak through the flan and make it soggy. This can be prevented by sprinkling cream stiffener evenly over the flan.

When Swiss roll breaks.
This is normally because the sponge has been overbaked. If the baking sheet with the sponge is placed into a preheated hot oven, 10 minutes of baking should suffice to cook it through. If the sponge is left in the oven for longer than necessary, it will dry out and break when rolled.

When your sponge cake is bumpy.
An evenly risen sponge depends on the right ingredients. Always use **half flour and half cornflour**. Cornflour can be replaced by a corresponding quantity of vanilla pudding powder. The sides of the springform pan must not be greased as this causes the sponge to slide down during baking, making the cake higher in the centre than at the sides.

When kneaded pastry breaks.
This usually means that too little liquid has been included in the pastry. This is easily solved. Simply make a depression in the centre of the pastry, pour in a little milk and work it in with a fork. The pastry will then be easier to knead.

When quark and oil pastry is too soft.
The quark was too wet. The quark available in the shops contains varying quantities of moisture. Allow quark to drain for a while to run off as much moisture as possible.

When egg-whites don't want to turn into "snow".
If even a tiny amount of yolk gets into the egg-whites during separation, it is almost impossible to beat the egg-whites stiffly. Any yolk should be removed, using the empty shell.

Storing

Storing cakes and biscuits.

A large variety of fine cakes, pastries and biscuits is still the high point of many a celebration during the year. Most cakes, etc. can be baked days or even weeks in advance and stored. If they have been properly packaged, they only need to be filled or decorated when the big day arrives and can be served fresh and crisp. Here are a few tips on how to treat various types of baked items to ensure they reach your table as fresh and aromatic as the day they were baked.

Cakes baked in a baking pan

Remove the cake from the oven at the end of the baking time and leave to stand for about 10 minutes (fruit cakes should be removed from the baking pan immediately) before turning out on to a wire rack. When thoroughly cooled off the cake can be stored wrapped in aluminium foil.

Flat cake, baked on a baking sheet

should be removed from the baking sheet while it is still warm. To do this cut the cake into quarters and leave to cool on a wire rack, otherwise the moisture will condense on the baking sheet and could impair the flavour of the cake.

Biscuits and cookies

These must all be removed from the baking sheet and cooled on a wire rack. When they are fully cooled they can be packed and stored. Biscuits must be stored cool and dry. Biscuits that are meant to stay crisp must be kept in tins with well fitting lids. Biscuits that are intended to soften should be left exposed to the air until they have the right texture. They are then stored in a loosely covered tin. Biscuits will stay soft if stored with a slice of bread. Different kinds of biscuits can be stored in the same tin. It is advisable to store them in layers separated by greaseproof paper or aluminium foil. Very spicy biscuits should be stored separately.

Macaroons

Macaroons should not be baked too long. They should still feel soft when removed from the oven. While they are cooling on the wire rack the macaroons dry out to the right texture. They will retain their outer crispness if stored in tightly sealed tins.

Stollen

Stollen is a type of sweet bread baked in Germany around Advent and Christmas. After it has been allowed to cool fully on a wire rack it can be wrapped in aluminium foil. If stored in a cool, dry place stollen will stay fresh for up to 4 weeks and the aroma of the fruit and spices will permeate the entire loaf.

Freezing cakes, pastries and doughs

Gateaux that have been decorated with fresh cream or other cream should be prefrozen and then packed, otherwise the decorations could be spoiled. When possible freeze cakes etc. in portions. Food that has been thawed should not be refrozen.

Storing

Food should not be stored for too long. Look upon 3–6 months as a maximum.
All dry cakes etc. can be thawed in the oven (e.g. butter or sugar cake, flan cases, deep fried cakes (e.g. doughnuts, piped biscuits). The same applies to sausage rolls, which can then be served hot from the oven.
Cakes and biscuits made with egg-whites (e.g. meringues and macaroons) are unsuitable for freezing.

Thawing time in the oven: 5–20 minutes; depending on the thickness of the food at room temperature: 3–4 hours.
Depending on their thickness and type etc., fruit-filled gateaux or cakes with fruit cream filling can take longer to thaw than those filled with cream only.
Cakes will cut best when semi-thawed.

Type of cake, etc.	**Freezing properties**	**Comments**
Stirred cake	good	Freeze without icing, brittle topping or fruit filling
Kneaded pastry/dough	good	Freeze without icing or fruit filling
Quark/oil Pastry/dough	good	Freeze without icing. Pastries (e.g. ham rolls) that are to be baked again should not be baked too brown the first time.
Sponge mixtures	good	Prefreeze butter cream or fresh cream sponges before packaging
Choux pastry	good	Freeze pastries ready cut. Reheat in the oven before filling.
Puff pastry	good	Freeze with or without filling.
Danish pastry	good	Freeze without icing. Can be thawed in the oven at 175° C, then iced
Yeast pastry/dough	good	Can be thawed in the oven at 175° C.
Deep fried pastries	good	Freeze without icing or icing sugar, can be thawed in the oven at 175° C and then iced or dusted.

Stirred cake mixtures

Preparation

Mixing flour and baking powder
If the recipe calls for baking powder or cocoa it should be mixed with the flour (unless making a marbled cake).

Sieving flour and baking powder together
Sieving the flour loosens it up and distributes the baking powder through it evenly. This makes the finished cake lighter. Wholemeal flour and baking powder are simply mixed. The coarser structure of the wholemeal flour does not allow clumping. This makes sieving unnecessary.
Baking pans that are to be used for stirred cake mixtures should be well greased by brushing with soft butter or margarine. Do not use oil as this would run down the edge of the pan.
If necessary the inside of the baking pan can also be sprinkled with breadcrumbs

Only grease the base of a springform pan.
Prepare the fruit as follows:
a) Pick over raisins and currants.
b) To peel almonds, first put them in boiling water for 2-3 minutes and leave to steep (remove pan from heat). Drain, peel and chop.

After loaf tins have been greased, they can be lined with greaseproof paper. This makes the cake easier to remove from the tin and keeps it fresh longer.
Prepare the paper lining as follows: Stand the tin on greaseproof paper and draw round the base, tip the tin up and draw round the side. Repeat for the other sides. Cut out the corners and fold along the base lines.

Method

"Cream the margarine (butter) until soft ..."
It is important that the fat should be neither too soft nor too hard. Fat that is too soft cannot be creamed. Fat that is too hard must be softened first. To do this, rinse out the mixing bowl with hot water and work the fat through thoroughly. When it is spreadable, beat it to a cream in about ½ a minute with an electric mixer on its highest setting.

"... Gradually add the sugar mixed with vanilla sugar to the creamed fat ..."
To do this, add the sugar to the fat a tablespoon at a time, beating each addition in thoroughly.

... when using honey. This should also be stirred in gradually.

Stirred cake mixtures

"... add the spices (baking oils, flavourings) ..."
Keep stirring until the mixture is fully homogeneous. Fine granulated sugar is preferable to coarse as it dissolves more easily.
If honey is used, the creamy sort (not too strongly crystallized) is better than the more liquid sort.

"... add eggs ..."
First break each egg into a cup to check that it is fresh. Never add all the eggs to the creamed fat and sugar (honey) mixture at once, as they will be very difficult to mix in.
Add eggs one at a time and stir for about ½ a minute until fully combined. It is important to stir the fat-sugar (honey)-egg mixture until it is completely smooth.

"... stir in the sieved flour and baking powder mixture ..."
Add the sieved flour and baking powder mixture a tablespoon at a time, using the medium setting on your electric mixer. If the mixture is too stiff add a little milk. Baking powder must not come into direct contact with liquid as this would make it start to rise prematurely. If you have to add milk or flour to adjust the mixture, stir it in quickly, otherwise the texture of the finished cake will be impaired (air bubbles). When the mixture is right stir it through on a medium setting.

"... only use enough milk to produce a heavy dropping mixture (mixture lifted on to a spoon must drop slowly) ..."

The amount of milk a mixture needs depends on the absorbency of the flour and the size of the eggs used. The mixture is right when it will drop heavily from a spoon. If too much milk is added the finished cake may contain water stripes. Stirred mixtures that contain high proportions of fat and eggs are an exception to this rule. They can be softer because the eggs will stiffen them up during baking.

"... prepare the fruit as instructed in the recipe and stir into the mixture ..."

Fruit should be stirred in on a medium setting. If stirred for too long the fruit can be crushed and the cake will turn a dirty grey colour.

"... pour the mixture into the prepared baking pan."

Using a spatula, pour the mixture into the prepared baking tin and smooth the surface. Baking tins should be filled to about ⅔ with mixture.

Baking stirred cake mixtures

All stirred cake mixtures should be baked according to the instructions in the appropriate recipe. Before removing the cake from the oven, always check to see whether it is cooked. To do this, stick a wooden skewer into the centre of the cake. If it comes out clean, the cake is done. Take it out of the oven and leave to stand for 5 – 10 minutes.

Turn the cake out on to a wire cake rack to cool off. If the cake is in a springform pan, loosen the edges of the cake with a knife blade before opening the springform pan (see sponge mixture, p. 87).

Chocolate log

(photo p. 44/45)

	For the mixture, cream
100 g soft margarine or butter	for about ½ minute with the electric mixer on its highest setting. Gradually add
150 g sugar	
1 pkt vanilla sugar	
salt	Keep stirring until you have a smooth mixture. Gradually add
3 eggs	beating in each egg for about ½ minute. Stir in
100 g grated chocolate	Mix together
50 g flour	
1 pkt chocolate pudding powder	
2 level tsp baking powder	Sieve and add to the mixture by the tablespoon, alternating with
2 tbs milk	Continue stirring on medium setting (adding only enough milk to give the mixture a heavy dropping consistency). Finally add
75g peeled, ground almonds	to the mixture. Pour into greased log shape baking pan (30 x 11 cm) and place on the wire shelf in the oven.
Electricity:	
Conventional	175 – 200 (preheated)
Convection	150 – 160 (cold)
Gas:	2 – 3 (cold)
Baking time:	50 – 60 minutes

	For the glaze, break
100 g plain chocolate	into small pieces and put into a small pan over a water bath with
a little coconut fat	Stir until melted and smooth. Use to glaze the cooled cake. Decorate with
40 g peeled, split almonds	
Tip:	The chocolate log is even juicier if it is glazed with apricot jam as soon as it comes out of the oven. To do this push 4 – 5 tbs apricot jam through a sieve, heat for a few moments, stirring continuously. Spread over the hot chocolate log. Leave to cool off completely before applying the chocolate glaze.

Fancy biscuits

	For the mixture, cream
375 g soft margarine or butter	for about ½ minute with the electric mixer on its highest setting. Gradually add
250 g sugar	
2 pkt vanilla sugar	
salt	Keep stirring until you have a smooth mixture. Sieve
500 g flour	Add ⅔ of the flour by the tablespoon, stirring in each addition thoroughly on medium setting. Put the mixture on to a pastry board and knead to a smooth pastry with the remaining flour and
125 g peeled, ground almonds	Put the rolls into a biscuit press and press out biscuits on to a baking sheet. If you wish you can sieve
10 g cocoa	and mix it with
10 g sugar	Knead this into ⅓ of the biscuit mix. Put dark and light mix into the biscuit press together for an attractive effect. Push the baking sheet with the biscuits into the oven.
Electricity:	
Conventional	175 – 200 (preheated)
Convection	160 – 170 (pre-heated)
Gas:	3 – 4 (cold)
Baking time:	10 – 15 minutes
Variations:	Put the mixture through a mincer with a special insert. Arrange on the baking sheet as straight biscuits, S-shapes or circles. When baked and cooled off, dip the ends in melted chocolate or brush half the biscuits with melted chocolate.

Lemon Quark Cake

(Photo p. 53)

	For the mixture, cream
125 g soft butter	for about ½ minute with the electric mixer on its highest setting. Gradually add
125 g sugar	
1 pkt vanilla sugar	Keep stirring until you have a smooth mixture. Gradually add
2 eggs	beating in each egg for about ½ minute. Mix together
125 g flour	
1 level tsp baking powder	Sieve and add to the mixture by the tablespoon. Put the mixture into a springform pan (about 28 cm diameter), smooth the top and place on the wire shelf in the oven.
Electricity:	
Conventional	175 – 200 (preheated)
Convection	160 – 170 (cold)
Gas:	3 – 4 (cold)
Baking time:	25 – 30 minutes When cold, slice the cake through once horizontally. For the filling, stir
2 pkt white powdered gelatine	into a pan containing
8 tbs cold water	Leave to swell for 10 minutes Beat together
2 egg yolks, 8 tbs lemon juice	
150 g sugar	
1 pkt vanilla sugar	until creamy. Stir in
500 g low fat quark	
500 g full fat quark	
grated rind of 1 lemon (untreated)	Heat the gelatine, stirring continuously, until it has dissolved completely. Stir in a little of the quark mixture and then mix with the remaining quark mixture. Whip
500 g (2 pots) cream	until stiff. Beat
2 egg-whites	until stiff. Fold these ingredients into the quark mixture. Put the lower half of the cake into a springform pan ring that has been lined with greaseproof paper. Pour in the quark mixture, smooth the surface. Cut the top half of the cake into 16 wedges and place these on top of the quark cream. Dust with
icing sugar	Refrigerate until the filling is firm.

Stirred cake mixtures

Nut mounds
(wholefood biscuits)

	For the mixture, cream
150 g soft butter or margarine	for about ½ minute with the electric mixer on its highest setting. Gradually add
200 g hazelnut purée (jar)	
sea salt	
150 g crushed candied fruit peel	Keep stirring until you have a smooth mixture. Gradually add
2 eggs	(takes about ½ minute per egg). Mix together
125 g buckwheat	
125 g spelt (both finely ground)	
1 level tsp baking powder	Stir in by the tablespoon with the mixer on a medium setting. Remove small mounds from the mixture with 2 teaspoons and place them on a baking sheet lined with greaseproof paper. Push a few split almonds taken from
30 g peeled, split almonds	into the mounds. Push the baking sheet into the oven.
Electricity:	
Conventional	175 – 200 (preheated)
Convection	150 – 160 (preheated)
Gas:	3 – 4 (preheated)
Baking time:	about 15 minutes

Grandma's nut cake

	For the mixture, grind
150 hazel nuts	and roast them lightly on a baking sheet in the oven. Finely chop
100 hazel nuts	Cream
275 g soft butter	for about ½ minute with the electric mixer on its highest setting. Gradually add
175 g sugar	
1 pkt vanilla sugar	Keep stirring until you have a smooth mixture. Gradually add
4 eggs	beating in each egg for about ½ minute. Mix together
200 g flour	
1 level tsp baking powder	Sieve and add to the mixture by the tablespoon. Add all the hazel nuts to the mixture, pour it into a greased loaf

	tin (30 x 11 cm) lined with greaseproof paper, and place on the wire shelf in the oven.
Electricity:	
Conventional	175 – 200 (preheated)
Convection	160 – 170 (cold)
Gas:	2 – 3 (cold)
Baking time:	60 – 70 minutes Remove the cake from the loaf tin while still hot, prick all over with a fork and brush with
5 tbs rum.	
	For the apricot glaze, push
4 tbs apricot jam	through a sieve, mix with
3 tbs water	and boil up. Brush the cake with this mixture and leave to cool thoroughly.
	For the glaze, break
100 g chocolate	into small pieces and place in a small dish in a hot water bath with
a little coconut fat	Stir until melted and smooth. Use to glaze the cold cake.

Waffles

	For the mixture, melt
125 g butter	Pour into a mixing bowl and leave to cool. Stir
250 g sugar	
1 pkt vanilla sugar	
salt	into the slightly hardened fat. Mix with the electric mixer on highest setting until the butter and sugar are a creamy white. Gradually stir in
2 eggs	(about ½ minute per egg). Sieve
250 g flour	and stir into the mixture alternately with
500 ml (½ l) milk	with the mixer on a medium setting. Grease a well heated waffle iron with a little
cooking oil	and quickly bake small portions of the mixture in it until golden brown. Take the baked waffles out of the iron and roll them into horns or tubes quickly before they cool off. To keep waffles crisp, store them in a tin with a well fitting lid.

Frankfurt ring cake

(photo p. 57)

	For the mixture, cream
100 g soft butter or margarine	for about ½ minute with the electric mixer on its highest setting. Gradually add
150 g sugar	
1 pkt vanilla sugar	
4 drops lemon baking oil or	
½ phial of rum flavouring	Keep stirring until you have a smooth mixture. Gradually add
3 eggs	beating in each egg for about ½ minute. Mix together
150 g flour	
50 g cornflour	
2 level tsp baking powder	Sieve and add to the mixture by the tablespoon. Put the mixture into a greased angel cake pan (about 20 cm diameter) and place on the wire shelf in the oven.
Electricity:	
Conventional	175 – 200 (preheated)
Convection	160 – 170 (cold)
Gas:	2 – 3 (cold)
Baking time:	35 – 45 minutes
	For the butter cream, prepare a pudding from
1 pkt vanilla pudding powder	
100 g sugar	
500 ml (½ l) cold milk	following the instruction on the packet, but use

Continued on page 58

	only 100 g sugar. Refrigerate, stirring occasionally. Cream
250 g butter	Add the pudding to the butter by the tablespoon (make sure that neither the butter nor the pudding is too cold as this could cause them to curdle).
	For the brittle, mix together
a little butter	
60 g sugar	
125 g peeled chopped almonds	Heat, stirring continuously, until the mixture has browned sufficiently. Spread it on to a piece of aluminium foil and leave to cool. Slice the cake through twice horizontally (photo 1). Spread the bottom layer with
red jam	Remodel the three layers into a ring with butter cream between them (photo 2). Cover the cake with cream, leaving some for decoration. Sprinkle with brittle (photo 3) and decorate with the remaining cream. Garnish with
cherries or red jam	The cake should be filled one day before it is eaten.
Variation:	Bake the cake in a springform tube pan with a diameter of 24 cm.

Fruit flan
(stirred cake mixture)

	For the mixture, cream
75 g soft butter or margarine	for about ½ minute with the electric mixer on its highest setting. Gradually add
75 g sugar	
1 pkt vanilla sugar	
salt	Keep stirring until you have a smooth mixture. Gradually add
2 eggs	beating in each egg for about ½ minute. Mix together
125 g flour	
1 level tsp baking powder	Sieve and add to the mixture gradually with
1 tbs milk	

	Pour the mixture into a flan tin (about 28 cm diameter) or into individual flan tins, smooth the surface and place the tin (tins) on the wire shelf in the oven.
Electricity:	
Conventional	175 – 200 (preheated)
Convection	160 – 170 (cold)
Gas:	3 – 4 (cold)
Baking time:	20 – 25 minutes
	For the filling, wash and drain
1 kg raw fruit (e.g. strawberries, raspberries, blackberries, red or black currants, kiwis, bilberries, grapes)	(only pick over raspberries). Remove any stalks. Peel, slice, etc. Sprinkle with
sugar	and leave to stand for a short time. Alternatively, drain any
stewed or preserved fruit	and arrange the fruit on the flan.
	For the jelly glaze, prepare
1 pkt of fruit jelly glaze	as described on the packet, using
sugar	
250 ml (¼ l) water or fruit juice	Pour over the fruit.

Crème Fraîche Waffles

	For the mixture, quickly beat
2 pots (150 g each) crème fraîche	for about ½ minute with the electric mixer on its highest setting. Gradually mix in
100 g sugar	
grated rind of ½ lemon (untreated)	
salt	Keep stirring until you have a smooth mixture. Gradually add
3 eggs	beating in each egg for about ½ minute. Mix together
250 g flour	
1 level tsp baking powder	Sieve and add to the mixture gradually on medium setting. Grease a waffle iron and bake small portions of the mixture in the iron until brown. Place on a wire rack to cool off.

Apple cake

(photo p. 61)

	For the mixture, cream
125 g soft butter or margarine	for about ½ minute with the electric mixer on its highest setting. Gradually add
125 g sugar	
1 pkt vanilla sugar	
salt	
4 drops lemon baking oil	Keep stirring until you have a smooth mixture. Gradually add
3 eggs	beating in each egg for about ½ minute. Mix together
200 g flour	
2 level tsp baking powder	Sieve and add to the mixture by the tablespoon alternating with
1 – 2 tbs milk	(use only enough milk to make a heavy dropping mixture). Grease the base of a springform pan (28 cm diameter) and pour in the mixture. Smooth the surface.
	For the topping, peel, core and quarter
750 g apples	Make cuts in each apple quarter (see photo p. 61) and arrange them in circles on the mixture. Put the baking pan on the wire shelf in the oven.
Electricity:	
Conventional	175 – 200 (preheated)
Convection	160 – 170 (cold)
Gas:	3 – 4 (cold)
Baking time:	40 – 50 minutes
	For the apricot glaze, push
2 tbs apricot jam	through a sieve, mix with
1 tbs water	and boil up. Brush the cake with this mixture as soon as it comes out of the oven.
Variation:	Replace the apples with 600 g stoned sour cherries.

Irish fruit cake
(wholefood cake)

	Pour
125 ml (1/8 l) whisky	over
200 g sultanas	
125 g currants	
100 g raisins	
100 g candied lemon peel	
100 g candied orange peel	Cover and leave to stand overnight.
	For the mixture, cream
300 g soft butter	for about ½ minute with the electric mixer on its highest setting. Gradually add
250 g honey	
pinch of sea salt	Keep stirring until you have a smooth mixture. Gradually add
6 eggs	beating in each egg for about ½ minute. Mix together
300 g finely milled wheat	
1 slightly rounded tsp baking powder	
100 g peeled, ground almonds	and add to the mixture by the tablespoon, adding the fruit at the end. Grease the base of a springform pan (22 cm diameter), put a double strip of aluminium foil around the inside walls, allowing it to extend 6 – 7 cm above the rim and pour in the mixture. Smooth the surface. Decorate the surface with
60 g peeled almonds	Put the baking pan on the wire shelf in the oven.
Electricity:	
Conventional	150 – 175 (preheated)
Convection	140 (cold)
Gas:	2 (cold)
Baking time:	2 – 2 ¼ hours Carefully remove the finished cake from the baking pan and strip off the aluminium foil.
	For the apricot glaze, push
3 tbs peach-apricot-maracuja jam (made with natural thickener)	through a sieve. Brush the cake with this mixture as soon as it comes out of the oven.

Nut florentine biscuits

	For the florentine mixture, roast
300 g hazel nuts	on a baking sheet in the preheated oven
Electricity:	200 – 225
Gas:	3 – 4
Baking time:	8 – 12 minutes
	Pour the roasted nuts into a colander and rub off the skins with your hands. Put
50 g honey	
150 g sugar	
250 ml (¼ l) double cream	into a pan, bring to the boil and boil for 5 – 6 minutes stirring continuously. Add the skinned hazelnuts
100 g peeled, chopped almonds	
grated peel of 1 lemon (untreated)	
ground cinnamon	
30 g flour	Stir, bring to the boil and remove from heat.
	Using a tablespoon, put mounds of the mixture on to greaseproof paper (about 1 ½ tbs per biscuit).
	Dampen hands with
milk	and carefully flatten the mounds, ensuring that the hazel nuts are evenly distributed. Push the baking sheet into the oven.
Electricity:	
Conventional	175 (preheated)
Convection	150 (preheated)
Gas:	2 (preheated)
Baking time:	about 20 minutes.
	Leave the biscuits to cool off on the baking sheet for about 10 minutes. Remove and allow to cool off completely.
	For the glaze, heat
200 g baking chocolate	in a small bowl in a water bath. Stir until smooth, allow to cool a little until it thickens, then reheat. Spread the chocolate fairly thickly on the reverse of the biscuits. Draw a wavy pattern in the chocolate with a fork, and allow to set.

Stirred cake mixtures

Light and airy quark cake
(photo p. 65)

	For the mixture, cream
175 g soft butter	for about ½ minute with the electric mixer on its highest setting. Gradually add
150 g sugar	
grated peel of 1 lemon (untreated)	
2 – 3 tbs lemon juice	Keep stirring until you have a smooth mixture. Gradually add
7 eggs	beating in each egg for about ½ minute. Stir in
750 g low fat quark	
75 g semolina	by the tablespoon, with the mixer on medium setting. Grease the base of a springform pan (28 cm diameter) and pour in the mixture. Smooth the surface and put into the oven on the wire shelf.
Electricity:	
Conventional	175 (preheated)
Convection	150 (cold)
Gas:	2 – 3 (cold)
Baking time:	about 70 minutes Leave the finished cake in the oven, with the door slightly open, for about 30 minutes. Remove and leave to cool completely in the baking pan.

Plum cake

	For the filling, wash, dry and stone
1 – 1 ¼ kg plums	
	For the mixture, cream
100 g soft butter	
100 g almond paste	for about ½ minute with the electric mixer on its highest setting. Gradually add
80 g sugar	
pinch of salt	
2 tbs grated lemon peel (untreated)	Keep stirring until you have a smooth mixture. Gradually add
3 eggs	beating in each egg for about ½ minute.

Continued page 66

	Mix together
200 g flour	
2 level tsp baking powder	Sieve and add to the mixture by the tablespoon. Stir in
2 tbs sour cream	Toast
50 g peeled, chopped almonds	in a frying pan with no fat, stirring until they are browned. Break them up between your fingers and sprinkle them over the greased base of a springform pan (28 cm diameter). Pour the cake mixture into the baking pan, smooth the surface and arrange the plums on it, very close together, like fish scales.
	For the almond mixture, slice
150 g unpeeled almonds	Bring to the boil
60 g butter or margarine	
60 g sugar	
2 tbs honey	
pinch of ground cinnamon	stirring constantly. Stir the almonds and
3 tsp flour	into the butter mixture, and bring to the boil again. Distribute the hot almond mixture over the plums, put the baking pan into the oven on the wire shelf.
Electricity:	
Conventional	200 (preheated)
Convection	160 – 170 (cold)
Gas:	3 – 4 (cold)
Baking time:	40 – 45 minutes Leave the finished cake to cool off in the pan, loosen the edge with a sharp knife, transfer to a cake plate.
Accompaniment:	Slightly sweetened double cream flavoured with slivovitz, dust with cocoa if liked.

Prince Regent Cake

	For the mixture, cream
250 g soft butter or margarine	for about ½ minute with the electric mixer on its highest setting. Gradually add
250 g sugar	
1 pkt vanilla sugar	
pinch of salt	Keep stirring until you have a smooth mixture.

	Gradually add
4 eggs	beating in each egg for about ½ minute. Mix together
200 g flour	
50 g cornflour	
1 level tsp baking powder	Sieve and add to the mixture by the tablespoon, with the mixer on a medium setting. Make 7 flans from the mixture by spreading about 2 tbs each of the mixture on to the greased bases of springform baking pans (28 cm diameter). Make sure that the mixture is not spread too thinly at the edges otherwise it will become too dark. Bake each flan on the wire shelf in the oven until golden.
Electricity:	
Conventional	175 – 200 (preheated)
Convection	160 – 170 (preheated)
Gas:	3 – 4 (preheated)
Baking time:	8 – 10 minutes
	Remove the flans from the baking pans as soon as they come out of the oven.
	For the butter cream, prepare a pudding from
1 pkt chocolate pudding powder	
100 g sugar	
500 ml (½ l) milk	following the instructions on the packet but using only 100 g sugar. Refrigerate, stirring occasionally. Cream
250 g butter	Add the pudding to the butter by the tablespoon (make sure that neither the butter nor the pudding is too cold as this could cause them to curdle). Spread the flans with the butter cream and layer on top of each other, finishing with a layer of cake.
	For the glaze, melt
150 g chocolate	
a little coconut fat	in a small bowl in a water bath, stirring until smooth. Use to glaze the cake.
Variation:	Put some of the butter cream into an icing bag and pipe decorations on to the cake. Garnish with chocolate shapes.

Lemon duchess biscuits

(photo p. 69)

	For the mixture, cream
250 g soft butter or margarine	for about ½ minute with the electric mixer on its highest setting. Gradually add
150 g icing sugar	
grated rind of 2 lemons (untreated)	
6 tbs lemon juice	Keep stirring until you have a smooth mixture. Gradually add
2 egg yolks	beating in each one for about ½ minute. Sieve
375 g flour	Fold into the mixture, a tablespoon at a time. Put the mixture into a piping bag and pipe rounds on to a baking sheet covered with greaseproof paper (photo 1). Flatten the rounds slightly. Push the baking sheet into the oven.
Electricity:	
Conventional	175 – 200 (preheated)
Convection	160 – 170 (preheated)
Gas:	3 – 4 (preheated)
Baking time:	12 – 15 minutes
	When cooled off spread the undersides of half of the biscuits with about
2 tbs lemon jam	(photo 2), and sandwich together with the other halves.
	For the glaze, melt
50 g chocolate glaze	
50 g plain cooking chocolate	in a small bowl in a water bath over low heat, stirring until smooth. Dip the biscuits in the glaze until half covered (photo 3).

Heavenly cake

	For the mixture, cream
250 g soft butter	for about ½ minute with the electric mixer on its highest setting. Gradually add
200 g sugar	
1 pkt vanilla sugar	
pinch of salt	Keep stirring until you have a smooth mixture. Gradually add
4 egg yolks	beating in each one for about ½ minute. Mix together
250 g flour	
2 level tsp baking powder	Sieve and add to the mixture by the tablespoon, using the mixer on medium setting. Stiffly beat
4 egg-whites	To make 4 layers, spread 2 tbs of mixture over each of 4 greased springform pan bases (28 cm diameter). Make sure the mixture is not spread too thinly at the edges, otherwise it will become too dark. Spread ¼ of the whipped egg-whites evenly on each layer. Mix together
50 g sugar	
1 pkt vanilla sugar	
1 level tsp cinnamon	Sprinkle ¼ of this mixture and ¼ of
100 g peeled, chopped almonds	over each layer. Bake each layer, without the springform ring, on the wire shelf until golden
	Electricity:
Conventional	175 – 200 (preheated)
Convection	160 – 170 (preheated)
Gas:	3 – 4 (preheated)
Baking time:	15 – 20 minutes
	Remove the flans from the baking pans as soon as they come out of the oven and transfer to a wire rack to cool.
	For the filling, wash, drain and trim
500 g blackcurrants	Sprinkle with
125 g sieved icing sugar	Beat
500 g (2 pots) double cream	for ½ minute, and sprinkle into it
3 pkt cream stiffener	Continue beating until the cream is stiff. Carefully fold the blackcurrants into the cream and spread over each cake layer. Layer the cake together, finishing with a layer of cake.

Grilled layer cake

	For the mixture, cream
250 g soft butter or margarine	for about ½ minute with the electric mixer on its highest setting. Gradually add
250 g sugar	
1 pkt vanilla sugar	
pinch of salt	
4 tbs rum	Keep stirring until you have a smooth mixture. Gradually add
2 eggs	
4 egg yolks	beating in each one for about ½ minute. Mix together
150 g flour	
100 g cornflour	
3 level tsp baking powder	Sieve and add to the mixture by the tablespoon, with the mixer on a medium setting. Stiffly beat
4 egg-whites	and fold into the mixture carefully on medium setting. Line the greased base of a loaf tin (35 x 11) with greaseproof paper. Using a brush, spread 1 well heaped tbs of mixture over the base. Bake the cake mixture under the preheated grill until brown (the distance between the mixture and the grill should be about 20 cm).
Grilling time	
Electricity:	about 2 minutes
Gas:	about 2 minutes Repeat the grilling process layer by layer until all the cake mixture has been used up (vary the shelf height so that the cake stays 20 cm from the grill). Carefully loosen the edges of the finished cake from the sides of the loaf tin and turn out onto a baking sheet. Remove the greaseproof paper and put the cake into the hot oven for a further 5 minutes.
	For the glaze, break
100 g chocolate	into small pieces, and melt in a small bowl with
25 g coconut fat	in a water bath, over a low heat, stirring continuously until the mixture is smooth. Use to glaze the cake when it has cooled off.

Dutch cake

(baked in a rosette or springform baking pan, photo p. 73)

	For the kneaded pastry, mix together
150 g flour	
½ level tsp baking powder	Sieve into a mixing bowl and add
50 g sugar	
1 pkt vanilla sugar	
salt	
1 egg	
75 g soft butter	Using the kneading attachment on the mixer, knead the ingredients on a low setting, switching to high. Remove from the mixing bowl and knead on the work surface until you have a smooth ball. Refrigerate for about 30 minutes. Roll the pastry out thinly and use it to line a springform pan (28 cm diameter, base greased). Sprinkle with
2 tbs breadcrumbs	(photo 1). Drain
500 g sour cherries (preserved)	and arrange on the pastry.
	For the cake mixture, cream
200 g almond paste	
175 g soft butter	for about ½ minute with the electric mixer on its highest setting. Gradually add
100 g sugar	
2 tbs "Kirsch"	Keep stirring until you have a smooth mixture. Gradually add
4 eggs	beating in each one for about ½ minute. Mix together
125 g flour	

Continued on page 74

1 level tsp baking powder	Sieve and add to the mixture by the tablespoon, with the mixer on a medium setting. Pour the mixture over the cherries (photo 2) and smooth the surface.
	Place the baking pan in the oven on the wire shelf.
	Electricity:
Conventional	175 – 200 (preheated)
Convection	160 (cold)
Gas:	3 – 4 (cold)
Baking time:	Approx. 1 hour
	For the glaze, sieve
125 g icing sugar	and mix with
2 tbs cherry juice	stirring until you have a thick mixture. Glaze the cake with this mixture (photo 3) and decorate the edge of the cake with
peeled, chopped almonds	
toasted almonds	

Canadian Apple Cake
(wholefood cake)

	For the mixture, cream
150 g soft margarine or butter	for about ½ minute with the electric mixer on its highest setting. Gradually add
75 – 100 g maple syrup seeds from 1 vanilla pod or the grated peel of one lemon (untreated)	
sea salt	Keep stirring until you have a smooth mixture. Gradually add
3 eggs	beating in each egg for about ½ minute. Mix together
50 g finely ground spelt or wheat 1 heaped tsp baking powder	
125 g fine porridge oats	and add to the mixture by the tablespoon. Pour ⅔ of the mixture into a springform baking pan or pie dish (28 cm diameter) and smooth the surface. Peel, quarter, core and chop
600 – 750 g soft apples	and distribute over the mixture, sprinkle with
50 g sultanas	Using 2 teaspoons, distribute the remaining mixture in heaps on the apples. Dot with
50 g butter	Sprinkle with

40 g peeled, flaked almonds	and place on the wire shelf in the oven.
Electricity:	
Conventional	175 – 200 (preheated)
Convection	160 (cold)
Gas:	3 – 4 (cold)
Baking time:	50 – 60 minutes

Pineapple and marzipan cake

	For the mixture, beat
200 g almond paste	Using an electric mixer, add
175 g soft margarine or butter	and keep mixing until you have a smooth mixture. Gradually add
175 g sugar	
1 pkt vanilla sugar	
salt	Keep stirring until you have a smooth mixture. Gradually add
3 eggs	beating in each egg for about ½ minute. Mix together
300 g flour	
2 heaped tsp baking powder	Sieve and stir in by the tablespoon with the mixer on a medium setting. Drain and cut into pieces
3 slices of pineapple (can)	and carefully fold into the mixture with the mixer on a medium setting. Pour the mixture into a greased loaf tin lined with greaseproof paper (30 x 11 cm) and place on the wire shelf in the oven.
Electricity:	
Conventional	175 – 200 (preheated)
Convection	160 – 170 (cold)
Gas:	3 – 4 (cold)
Baking time:	60 – 70 minutes
	For the glaze, break
100 g plain chocolate	into small pieces and melt in a small bowl in a water bath together with
a little coconut fat	until smooth. Use to glaze the cooled cake. Decorate with
pieces of pineapple	

Stirred cake mixtures

English biscuits
(photo p. 77)

	For the mixture, cream together
100 g almond paste	
250 g butter	with an electric mixer. Keep mixing until you have a smooth mixture. Gradually add
100 g cane sugar	Keep stirring until you have a smooth mixture. Sieve
250 g flour	
2 heaped tsp baking powder	Sieve and stir in by the tablespoon with the mixer on a medium setting. Shape the mixture into a roll and refrigerate for 2 – 3 hours. Roll out the pastry about 1 – 1 ½ cm thick and cut into strips 1 ½ x 6 cm. Place on a well greased baking sheet. Decorate each biscuit with a fork, sprinkle with
cane sugar or sugar	and bake in the oven
Electricity:	
Conventional	150 – 175 (preheated)
Convection	140 – 150 (preheated)
Gas:	2 – 3 (preheated)
Baking time:	25 – 30 minutes

Viennese sand cake

	For the mixture, remove 2 tsp egg-white from
6 eggs	and cover and reserve. Whisk the eggs on the highest mixer setting, gradually adding
375 g finely granulated sugar	
2 pkt vanilla sugar	Beat for 1 ½ to 2 minutes. Add
2 tbs water	
175 g flour	mixed and sieved with
175 g cornflour	
1 ½ level tsp baking powder	Stir in a tablespoon at a time. Carefully stir in
375 g hot (not boiling) butter	Place a greased flower-shaped mould on the ring of a springform baking pan, pour in the mixture and push the ring and mould on to the wire shelf in the centre of the oven. Alternatively, pour the mixture into a springform baking pan (28 cm diameter, base greased) and push into the

Continued on page 78

	the oven on the wire shelf.
Electricity:	
Conventional	150 – 175 (preheated)
Convection	140 – 150 (cold)
Gas:	2 – 3 (cold)
Baking time:	70 minutes
	Turn the cake out on to a cake rack and leave to cool off slightly.
	For the apricot glaze, push
3 heaped tbs apricot jam	through a sieve. Mix with
3 tbs apricot brandy	
1 tbs water	
1 tsp rum	Bring to the boil and use to coat the sand cake.
	For the glaze, sieve
30 g icing sugar	into the reserved
2 tsp egg-white	
a little water	Stir until you have a mixture that will allow itself to be piped. Pour the mixture into a greaseproof paper piping bag, cut off the tip and decorate the cake with the glaze.

"Heidesand"

	Melt and brown
250 g butter	Pour into a mixing bowl and leave to stand until solid again. With an electric mixer, beat the butter for about ½ a minute until creamy. Gradually add
200 g sugar	
1 pkt vanilla sugar	
2 – 3 tbs milk	Continue stirring until the mixture is white and creamy.
	Sieve together
375 g flour	
1 level tsp baking powder	Add ⅔ of the flour to the mixture by the tablespoon. Turn out on to the work surface and knead to a smooth dough with the remaining flour. Shape the dough into rolls with a diameter of 3 cm, refrigerate until firm, cut into slices ½ cm thick, arrange on a baking sheet and bake.
Electricity:	
Conventional	175 – 200 (preheated)
Convection	160 – 170 (preheated)
Gas:	2 – 3 (preheated)
Baking time:	10 – 15 minutes

Crumble cake with apple filling

	For the mixture, cream
250 g soft margarine or butter	for about ½ minute with the electric mixer on its highest setting. Gradually add
200 g sugar	
1 pkt vanilla sugar	
salt	Keep stirring until you have a smooth mixture. Add
1 egg	beating in for about ½ minute. Sieve together
500 g flour	
1 pkt baking powder	Stir half the flour into the mixture a tablespoon at a time, using the mixer on a medium setting. Add the remaining flour and mix in using the kneading attachment until you have a crumble-like mixture.
	For the filling, peel, quarter, core and chop
1 ½ – 2 kg apples	Mix with
1 tbs water	
50 – 75 g sugar	
pinch of ground cinnamon	
75 g cleaned raisins	Simmer for a while, stirring constantly. Leave to cool, add
sugar	to taste if necessary. Put half the crumble mixture on a greased baking sheet, pressing it down firmly, and pushing it upwards by about ½ cm at the edges. Place a folded strip of aluminium foil along the edge of the pastry. Distribute the apple filling evenly over the pastry, sprinkle with the remaining crumble mixture and bake.
Electricity:	
Conventional	175 – 200 (preheated)
Convection	160 – 170 (cold)
Gas:	3 – 4 (cold)
Baking time:	35 – 45 minutes
Tip:	This cake can be baked a day in advance.

Stirred cake mixtures

King cake

	For the mixture, cream
250 g soft margarine or butter	for about ½ minute with the electric mixer on its highest setting. Gradually add
200 g sugar, 1 pkt vanilla sugar ½ phial lemon-flavoured baking oil or 1 phial rum-flavoured baking oil	
salt	Keep stirring until you have a smooth mixture. Add
5 eggs	beating in each egg separately for about ½ minute. Sieve together
500 g flour 4 levels tsp baking powder	Stir half the flour into the mixture a tablespoon at a time, alternating with milk taken from
125 ml (⅛ l) milk	(use only enough milk to make a heavy dropping mixture). Add
125 g currants 375 g raisins 100 g finely chopped candied lemon peel	folding them in carefully with the mixer on medium setting. Pour the mixture into a greased loaf tin (35 x 11 cm) lined with greaseproof paper, place the loaf tin on the wire shelf in the oven, and bake.
Electricity:	
Conventional	175 – 200 (preheated)
Convection	160 – 170 (cold)
Gas:	2 – 3 (cold)
Baking time:	80 – 100 minutes

Marble cake

	For the mixture, cream
300 g soft margarine or butter	for about ½ minute with the electric mixer on its highest setting. Gradually add
275 g sugar, 1 pkt vanilla sugar 1 phial of rum-flavoured baking oil	
salt	Keep stirring until you have a smooth mixture. Add
5 eggs	beating in each egg separately for about ½ minute. Sieve together
375 g flour	

4 level tsp baking powder	Stir half the flour into the mixture a tablespoon at a time, alternating with milk taken from
3 tbs milk	(use only enough milk to make a heavy dropping mixture). Pour ⅔ of the mixture into a greased deep baking pan (24 cm diameter). Sieve
20 g cocoa	and mix with
20 g sugar	
2 – 3 tbs milk	Stir into the remaining mixture until it drops heavily from a spoon. Pour the dark mixture over the light one. Pull a fork through the two layers of cake mixture using a spiral motion. This gives the marbled effect. Put the baking pan on the wire shelf in the oven and bake.
Electricity:	
Conventional	175 – 200 (preheated)
Convection	160 – 170 (cold)
Gas:	2 – 3 (cold)
Baking time:	50 – 65 minutes
	Dust the cake with
icing sugar	

Napoleon cake

	For the mixture, cream
300 g soft margarine or butter	for about ½ minute with the electric mixer on its highest setting. Gradually add
125 g sugar	
1 phial of rum-flavoured baking oil	Add
7 eggs	beating in each egg separately for about ½ minute. Sieve together
150 g flour	
1 pkt baking powder	Stir into the mixture a tablespoon at a time on medium setting. Stir in
150 g ground hazel nuts	
150 chocolate flakes	on a medium setting. Pour the mixture into a greased deep baking pan (24 cm diameter). Put the baking pan on the wire shelf in the oven and bake.
Electricity:	
Conventional	175 (preheated)
Convection	150 (cold)
Gas:	3 (cold)
Baking time:	Approx. 65 minutes.

Sponge cake mixtures

Preparation

Hazel nuts and almonds should be prepared as directed in the chapter on stirred cake mixtures on page 46.

When baking sponge cakes always line the base of the baking pan and the baking sheet with greaseproof paper (sections a – c).

It is advisable to line baking pans and baking sheets with greaseproof paper.

a) To make a paper liner for a springform baking pan: turn the baking pan upside down. Place the paper on top and cut off the paper which projects past the edge of the baking pan with a sharp knife.

b) Greasing the baking pan.
Using a brush, dot soft butter or margarine on to the base of the pan in 4 places. **Do not grease the edges.**

c) Line the base of the pan with the paper, pressing it down firmly. To do this assemble the springform pan, take the paper across the pan from one side to the other, smoothing it to make sure no wrinkles or bumps form.

The individual steps

"...whisk eggs..."
Eggs used for baking should always be fresh. Even so, it is wise to break each egg individually into a cup to check that it is good. A bad egg, added last, will ruin the mixture.

"...and hot water for about 1 minute until fluffy..."
Add the water to the egg. If the recipe gives an approximate amount of water, adjust it to the size of the eggs. For small eggs use more, for large eggs less water.

Sponge cake mixtures

"...whisk in the sugar or honey mixed with vanilla sugar gradually in about 1 minute. Continue whisking for a further 2 minutes. Add the flavouring to the creamy egg mixture..."
Switch off mixer.

"...sieve half the flour, baking powder and cornflour mixture over the eggs and fold in quickly on a low setting. Work in the remaining flour in the same way..."
Mixing and sieving the flour works air into it and distributes the cornflour (pudding powder, cocoa) and baking powder evenly. This will give you a lighter textured sponge cake.

If using **wholemeal flour** the flour, mixed with baking powder, must be folded in in two stages using the lowest mixer setting.

"...pour the mixture into the baking pan (sheet) which has been lined with greaseproof paper."
It is best to use a spatula to scrape the mixture into the prepared baking pan and smooth the surface.

Baking sponge mixtures

Sponge mixtures must be baked as instructed in the recipe as soon as they have been prepared as otherwise they will collapse. Always check whether the cake is done before removing it from the oven. To do this, put the flat of your hand on the cake and press gently. If cooked it should not feel moist but should have a soft, cotton wool feel to it. Sponge cake which is baked for too long is hard and dry.

When the sponge has cooled slightly, loosen the edges with a knife and remove the springform ring.

Turn the cake out on to a cake rack and remove the baking paper at once to allow it to dry off. If you do not intend to use the sponge the same day, the paper can be left on.

Filling sponges.

Lay the sponge cake on a piece of greaseproof paper with the smooth, flat, base facing upwards. It can then be sliced through with a large knife or a piece of thread. To make sure that the cake is cut into equal halves, use a small pointed knife to make a cut about 1 cm deep all round the cake.

Lay a piece of thread into the cut, take hold of both ends, cross them over and pull firmly. The thread will cut through the cake.

Lift off the top layer with a piece of paper to stop it from breaking. To do this push the paper, angled down, between the cake layers. Pull it through using both hands, holding back the top layer of cake with your index fingers if it starts to move.

Lift off the top layer taking care to keep the paper straight as the cake could otherwise break.

If you want to halve the cake with a knife, it is best to use a knife which is longer than the diameter of the cake.

For filling you can use butter cream made with pudding powder, prepacked cake cream powder or jam. If using butter cream it makes a nice change to alternate it with a layer of jam. Use a knife, a spatula or a palette knife to spread a filling.

The layers of sponge can be put together again with the aid of the paper, taking care that the edges meet exactly.

Spread butter cream on the next layer and put the third layer on top.

Spread the top and sides of the cake with butter cream, using a dinner knife to spread the cream around the sides.

Decorating the filled cake

Decorate the sides of the cake with chocolate flakes, flaked almonds or toasted oatmeal. To do this sprinkle the decoration closely around the edge of the cake and then push up with a spatula or pastry scraper.

Before decorating the top of the cake, mark it into sections with a special slice marker.

When decorating always keep the icing bag vertical, holding it shut with your right hand and twisting to press out the cream (butter cream). The left hand guides the bag. Do not use the whole hand but only thumb and index finger to guide the nozzle. The heat of your hand could make the cream too liquid. The butter cream sponge in the photo is decorated with question marks piped close to each other. As soon as one has been piped, take the nozzle back a little way before piping the next question mark on the bottom part of the previous one. Pipe circles in the centre of the cake and garnish with chocolate shapes.

To make butter cream horns, start piping from the centre making loops close together, which get bigger towards the edge of the cake. Pipe a rosette in the centre. Put a glace cherry in each horn. The edge of the cake has been sprinkled with flaked, toasted almonds.

For this cream cake a question mark has been piped at the edge of each slice, with a rosette piped on the end. A circle has been piped in front of each question mark and decorated with a piece of strawberry. The edge of the cake is decorated with chopped pistachio nuts.

This butter cream cake has been decorated with stars of different sizes. They get smaller from the edge to the centre where they come together to form a circle. Garnish with chocolate decorations. Cocoa is sprinkled in the centre. The edge of the cake is sprinkled with grated chocolate.

Sponge cake mixtures

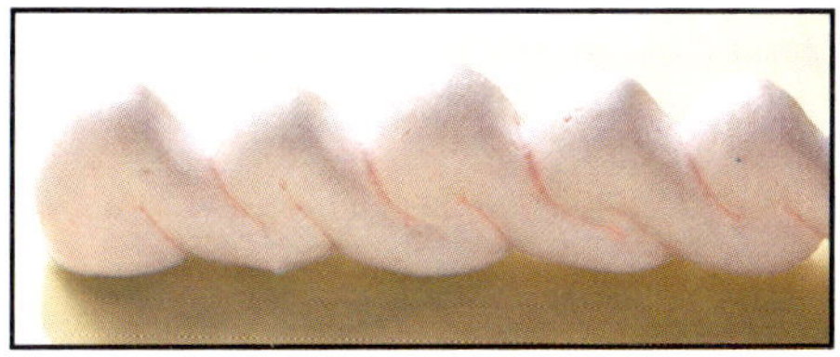

The cream for this cake has been coloured with fruit juice or food colouring. Using a smooth nozzle a ring of almost vertical waves has been piped round the edge. The decoration changes to tilted circles and blobs towards the centre. The centre and edges of the cake are sprinkled with desiccated coconut.

The top of this cream cake has been decorated with flan jelly on which a flower pattern has been piped. The centres of the flowers are decorated with a little of the red jelly. The edge of the cake is decorated with piped cream.

To make this cake knead together almond paste with icing sugar (75 g of icing sugar for each 200 g almond paste). Roll out the paste and cut out a sheet the size of the cake and a strip as wide as the sides. Cover the cake with these. Make a thin icing from sieved icing sugar mixed with egg-white and coloured with a little green food colouring. Brush this over the cake. Pipe on designs and decorate with small Easter eggs and coloured almond paste leaves.

Glazing sponge cakes

Before applying a glaze, spread the cake with jam to stop the glaze from soaking into the cake. Use a smooth jelly, rather than a jam which contains pieces of fruit (otherwise, push the jam through a sieve before use).
Pour the glaze into the centre of the cake.

Using a large knife quickly spread the glaze over the cake so that it runs down the sides. Keep the knife at a slight angle and use very little pressure. If the direction of the knife has to be changed, do not pull it out of the glaze as this could cause crumbs to be pulled out of the cake which would make the glaze look unattractive.
Using a knife held at an angle spread the glaze which has run down evenly around the sides.

It is important to transfer the cake as quickly as possible to a cake stand with the aid of a large knife. To do this, first loosen the cake from the cake board on which it has been glazed. Tip the board slightly and use the knife to slide the cake carefully on to the cake stand.

A few things to know about making a Swiss roll.

Line the baking sheet with greaseproof paper, first brushing three or four dabs of butter or margarine onto the baking sheet. Lay the paper on the sheet and press down firmly. Make a pleat in the paper at the open edge of the baking sheet to make a standing edge (to stop the cake mixture from spreading). Spread the cake mixture about 1 cm thick over the prepared paper.

As soon as the cake comes out of the oven, take a knife and loosen the edges away from the paper and baking sheet. With the aid of the paper lift the cake and turn it on to a kitchen towel which has been sprinkled with sugar.

Carefully brush the greaseproof paper with cold water and pull it off carefully and quickly.

Immediately spread the cake with jam. It is advisable to distribute the quantity of jam specified in the recipe over the cake and then spread it out with a pastry scraper.

Quickly roll up the Swiss roll.
Speed is of the essence here because if the sponge is allowed to cool off too much it is more likely to break when being handled. The kitchen towel is a help in rolling up the sponge.

Strawberry cream cake

(photo p. 82/83)

	For the mixture, whisk
2 eggs	
2 – 3 tbs hot water	for about 1 minute, until fluffy, using an electric mixer on its highest setting. Mix together
100 sugar	
1 pkt vanilla sugar	Stir in in about 1 minute then whisk for a further 2 minutes. Mix together
75 g flour	
50 g cornflour	
1 level tsp baking powder	Sieve half of the flour over the eggs and fold in quickly on lowest setting. Fold in the remaining flour in the same way. Pour the mixture into a springform baking pan (28 cm diameter, base greased and lined with greaseproof paper), put the baking pan on the wire shelf in the oven and bake.
Electricity:	175 – 200 (preheated)
Gas:	3 – 4 (cold)
Baking time:	20 – 30 minutes Turn the cake out of the baking pan and leave to cool off.
	For the filling prepare a cream from
1 pkt vanilla pudding powder	
25 g sugar	
just under 250 ml (¼ l) milk	following the instructions on the packet (but using only ¼ l milk). Leave to cool stirring occasionally. Wash, drain well and trim
500 g strawberries	Whisk
500 g (2 pots) double cream	for ½ minute. Sieve together
50 g icing sugar	
1 pkt vanilla sugar	
1 pkt cream stiffener	Sprinkle into the cream and whisk until stiff. Slice through the sponge cake once. Spread the pudding cream on the lower layer and cover with the strawberries. Spread ¾ of the cream over the strawberries and cover with the top layer of sponge. Cover the edges and top of the cake with the remaining cream and decorate with
strawberry halves.	

Sponge cake mixtures

Apricot cream cake

	For the kneaded pastry, mix together
150 g flour	
40 g sugar	
1 pkt vanilla sugar	Sieve into a mixing bowl and add
100 g soft butter	Using the kneading attachment on the mixer, knead the ingredients on a low setting, switching to high. Remove from the mixing bowl and knead on the work surface until you have a smooth ball. Refrigerate for a while. Roll the pastry out thinly and use it to line a springform pan (28 cm diameter, base greased). Prick several times with a fork and bake in the springform pan on the wire shelf in the oven.
Electricity:	
Conventional	200 – 225 (preheated)
Convection	About 170 (preheated)
Gas:	3 – 4 (preheated)
Baking time:	About 15 minutes
	When baking is finished loosen the pastry from the base of the springform pan, allow to cool then transfer to a cake stand.
	For the sponge mixture, whisk
3 eggs	
3-4 tbs hot water	for about 1 minute, until fluffy, using an electric mixer on its highest setting. Mix together
125 sugar	
1 pkt vanilla sugar	Stir in in about 1 minute then whisk for a further 2 minutes. Mix together
75 g flour	
75 g cornflour	
15 g cocoa	
2 level tsps baking powder	Sieve half of the flour over the eggs and fold in quickly on lowest setting. Fold in the remaining flour in the same way working in
75 g melted, cooled butter	Pour the mixture into a springform baking pan (28 cm diameter, base greased and lined with greaseproof paper), put the baking pan on the wire shelf in the oven and bake.
Electricity:	175 – 200 (preheated)

Gas:	3 – 4 (cold)
Baking time:	20 – 30 minutes Turn the cake out of the baking pan and leave to cool off. Slice through once.
	For the filling, drain
1 kg apricots (stewed or canned)	Reserve 12 apricot halves and cut the rest into small pieces. Make up the juice to 250 ml (¼ l) with water. Take 4 tbs of the juice and stir in
30 g cornflour	
25 g sugar	Bring the remaining juice to the boil, remove from the heat and stir in the cornflour mixture. Return to heat and bring back to the boil for a moment. Stir in the pieces of apricot and leave to cool. Stir in
2 tbs lemon juice	Whisk
500 g (2 pots) double cream	for ½ minute. Sieve together
50 g icing sugar	
2 pkts cream stiffener	Sprinkle into the cream and whisk until stiff. Fold half the whipped cream into the cold apricot mixture. Spread the pastry base with
3 tbs apricot jam	Place the lower half of the sponge cake on top. Spread with the apricot cream mixture, cover with the top layer of sponge and press down firmly. Spread the top and sides of the cake evenly with some of the remaining cream. Mark the top layer into 12 slices and decorate with the remaining cream. Stir
½ tsp white gelatine powder	into
1 tbs apricot juice or water	Leave to stand for 10 minutes until swollen. Heat, stirring continuously until the gelatine has dissolved. Brush the apricot halves with this mixture and use to decorate the cake. Sprinkle the sides of the cake with
60 g peeled, chopped, toasted almonds	

Sponge cake mixtures

Swiss cherry cake

	For the sponge mixture whisk
4 egg yolks, 1 egg-white	
2 – 3 tbs hot water	for about 1 minute, until fluffy, using an electric mixer on its highest setting. Mix together
100 sugar	
1 pkt vanilla sugar	Stir in in about 1 minute then whisk for a further 2 minutes. Mix together
75 g flour	
50 g cornflour	
1 level tsp baking powder	Sieve half of the flour over the eggs and fold in quickly on lowest setting. Fold in the remaining flour in the same way. Pour the mixture into a springform baking pan (28 cm diameter, base greased and lined with greaseproof paper), put the baking pan on the wire shelf in the oven and bake.
Electricity:	175 – 200 (preheated)
Gas:	3 – 4 (cold)
Baking time:	25 – 30 minutes
	Turn the cake out of the baking pan and leave to cool off.
	For the meringue whisk
3 egg-whites until stiff	gradually beat in
150 g sugar	
1 pkt vanilla sugar	Fold in
100 g peeled, ground almonds	Prepare 2 meringue layers from this mixture. To do this divide the mixture into two and put into two springform baking pans (28 cm diameter, bases greased and lined with greaseproof paper), put the baking pans on the wire shelf in the oven and bake.
Electricity:	
Conventional	100 – 110 (preheated)
Convection	100 – 110 (cold)
Gas:	1, turn off the oven after 30 – 40 minutes leaving the meringue layers in the oven for a further 20 minutes.
Baking time:	About 1 ½ hours
	As soon as the layers are baked, dampen the paper with water and remove it. Leave the layers to dry in the turned off oven for a further 15 – 20 minutes. Store the meringue layers in a pan with a well fitting lid to prevent them from softening.

	For the butter cream, prepare a pudding from
1 pkt raspberry-flavoured pudding powder	
75-100 g sugar	
500 ml (½ l) milk	following the instructions on the packet (but using only 75 – 100 g sugar). Leave to cool, stirring occasionally. Beat
250 g butter	until creamy, add the pudding by the spoonful (neither butter not pudding should be too cold as this would cause curdling).
	To soak the sponge cake, boil up
6 tbs water	
60 g sugar	Leave to cool. Add
6 tbs Kirsch	Spread butter cream on one of the meringue layers. Place the sponge cake on top, sprinkle with the Kirsch and spread with half the remaining butter cream. Place the second meringue layer on top and press down firmly. Use the remaining cream to coat the top and sides of the cake. Toast
50 g flaked almonds	in the oven, turning occasionally, until golden. Leave to cool. Sprinkle on the sides of the cake. Dip a knife in hot water and make a grid pattern on the cake. Just before the cake is served, dust it with
25 g icing sugar	The cake is easier to cut if it is filled a day in advance.

Chocolate fingers

	For the mixture, beat
1 egg	
1 egg yolk	
125 g sugar	
1 pkt vanilla sugar	
salt	
1 level tsp instant coffee powder	until fluffy, using an electric mixer on a medium setting. Break
60 g plain chocolate	into small pieces and melt in a small bowl in a water bath over a low heat. Stir until smooth, leave to cool off and stir into the egg mixture.

	Mix together
200 g unpeeled, ground almonds	
pinch of baking powder	Stir ⅔ of this into the egg mixture and knead in the rest. Refrigerate.
	For the glaze, whisk
1 egg-white	until stiff. Sieve
60 g icing sugar	Add to the egg-whites by the spoonful. Roll out the pastry into a rectangle (12x40 cm), spread the glaze evenly over the pastry, cut into fingers (6x1 cm) and bake in the oven on a greased baking sheet.
Electricity:	
Conventional	175 – 200 (preheated)
Convection	160 – 170 (preheated)
Gas:	3 – 4 (preheated)
Baking time:	10 – 15 minutes.

Fruity poppy seed cake

	Peel, quarter, core and chop
700 g apples	Whisk together
8 egg whites	
5 tbs cold water	until stiff, slowly beat in
300 g creamy honey	Mix together
grated rind of ½ lemon (untreated)	
8 egg yolks	Fold carefully into the egg-white mixture. Mix together
200 g ground hazel nuts	
250 g freshly ground poppy seeds	
50 g buckwheat flour	
1 rounded tsp baking powder	Fold in the ingredients one after another ending with the chopped apple. Pour the mixture into a springform baking pan (28 cm diameter, base greased and lined with greaseproof paper), smooth the surface and bake on the wire shelf of the oven
Electricity:	
Conventional	175 (preheated)
Convection	150 (cold)
Gas:	2 – 3 (cold)
Baking time:	55 – 60 minutes.

Sponge cake mixtures

Nut cake with vanilla cream

	For the mixture, whisk
7 eggs, 1 egg-white	for about 1 minute, until fluffy, using an electric mixer on its highest setting. Mix together
175 g sugar	
1 pkt vanilla sugar	
pinch of ground cinnamon	
salt	Stir in in about 1 minute then whisk for a further 2 minutes. Add
325 g ground hazel nuts	to the egg mixture. Fold in quickly on lowest mixer setting. Put
50 g sponge fingers	into a plastic bag, seal it and crush the biscuits with a rolling pin. Mix with
1 tsp baking powder	and add to the other ingredients. Carefully mix the ingredients. Pour the mixture into a springform baking pan (28 cm diameter, base greased and lined with greaseproof paper), put the baking pan on the wire shelf in the oven and bake.
Electricity:	175 (preheated)
Gas:	3 (cold)
Baking time:	45 – 50 minutes Remove from the baking pan and leave to cool. Slice through twice.
	For the filling, prepare a pudding from
1 pkt vanilla-flavoured pudding powder	
1 tbs sugar	
125 ml (⅛ l) cold milk	Stir in
1 pot crème fraîche	
1 egg yolk	Bring to the boil beating continuously. Stir in
30 g soft butter	Leave to cool, stirring occasionally. Spread the bottom and middle sponge layers with the cream and put them together again. Cover with the top layer. Push
3 – 4 tbs apricot jam	
	through a sieve and bring to the boil with
3 – 4 tbs rum or brandy	Brush the cake with this mixture and sprinkle the top and sides of the cake with
75 g ground hazel nuts or almonds.	
	Leave the cake for a while to allow to soak through.

Buckwheat cake
(wholefood cake)

	For the mixture, whisk
6 eggs	
2 tbs hot water	for about 1 minute, until fluffy, using an electric mixer on its highest setting. Beat in
125 g honey	
grated peel of ½ lemon (untreated)	for about 2 minutes. Fold in ⅓ of
175 g finely milled buckwheat	to the egg mixture using a low mixer setting, then add the remaining buckwheat. Pour the mixture into a springform baking pan (28 cm diameter, base greased and lined with greaseproof paper), put the baking pan on the wire shelf in the oven and bake.
Electricity:	175 - 200 (preheated)
Gas:	3 – 4 (cold)
Baking time:	30 – 35 minutes
	Remove from the baking pan and leave to cool. Slice through twice.
	For the filling, mix together
1 pkt white gelatine powder	
4 tbs cold water	Leave to swell for 10 minutes. Heat, stirring continuously until the gelatine has dissolved. Stir in
2 – 3 tbs lemon juice	Whisk
750 g (3 pots) double cream	until stiff, beat in the lukewarm gelatine solution and
6 tbs maple syrup	Put ¼ of the cream into an icing bag with a star shaped nozzle. Spread the lower cake layer with half of
350 g cranberry jam (jar, sweetened with honey)	Cover with ⅓ of the cream, cover firmly with the second sponge layer. Brush with the remaining jam (reserving about ½ tbs for decoration). Spread with half the remaining cream and cover with the last sponge layer. Spread the remaining cream over the top and sides of the cake and decorate the top with the cream in the icing bag. Decorate with the remaining jam or fresh cranberries immediately before serving.

Black Forest Gateau

	For the kneaded pastry, mix together
125 g flour	
10 g cocoa	
pinch of baking powder	Sieve into a mixing bowl and add
50 g sugar	
1 pkt vanilla sugar	
100 g soft butter or margarine	Using the kneading attachment on the mixer, knead the ingredients on a low setting, switching to high. Remove from the mixing bowl and knead on the work surface until you have a smooth ball. Refrigerate for a while. Roll the pastry out thinly and use it to line a springform pan (28 cm diameter, base greased). Prick several times with a fork and bake in the springform pan on the wire shelf in the oven.
Electricity:	
Conventional	200 – 225 (preheated)
Convection	170 (cold)
Gas:	3 – 4 (preheated)
Baking time:	About 15 minutes When baking is finished loosen the pastry from the base of the springform pan, allow to cool then transfer to a cake stand.
	For the sponge mixture, whisk
4 eggs	
2 tbs hot water	for about 1 minute, until fluffy, using an electric mixer on its highest setting. Mix together

Continued on page 108

Sponge cake mixtures

100 g sugar	
1 pkt vanilla sugar	Stir in in about 1 minute then whisk for a further 2 minutes. Mix together
75 g flour	
30 g cornflour	
10 g cocoa	
2 good pinches of ground cinnamon	
½ level tsp baking powder	Sieve half of the flour over the eggs and fold in quickly on lowest setting. Fold in the remaining flour in the same way. Pour the mixture into a springform baking pan (28 cm diameter, base greased and lined with greaseproof paper), put the baking pan on the wire shelf in the oven and bake.
Electricity:	175 – 200 (preheated)
Gas:	3 – 4 (cold)
Baking time:	25 – 30 minutes
	Turn the cake put of the baking pan and leave to cool.
	For the filling, drain
720 g stoned sour cherries (jar)	or wash and stone
750 g sour cherries	Mix with
75 g sugar	Leave to stand for a while to draw the juice. Bring to the boil for a moment, drain and leave to cool. Measure off 250 ml (¼ l) juice (make up with water if necessary). Mix
30 g cornflour	with 4 tbs of the juice. Bring the remaining juice to the boil, remove from the heat, stir in the cornflour mixture, return to heat and boil up again briefly. Stir in the cherries, leave the mixture to cool. Add
about 25 g sugar	
3 tbs Kirsch	to taste. Whisk
750 g (3 pots) double cream	for ½ minute. Sieve
50 g icing sugar	and mix with
1 pkt. vanilla sugar	
3 pkts cream stiffener	Whisk the cream until stiff. Spread half the cherries over the short pastry base, followed by ⅓ of the cream (photo 1). Slice the sponge cake through once and place one half on top of the cream. Press on firmly, spread with half the remaining cream and cover with the final sponge layer. Spread the cream evenly around the sides of the cake and pile it on the top (photo 2).
	Sprinkle the cake with
30 g grated chocolate	(photo 3).
Variation	Do not pile the remaining cream on to the top, spread some of it on evenly and use the rest to decorate the cake.

Nougat and almond biscuits

	For the mixture, whisk
4 eggs	for about 1 minute, until fluffy, using an electric mixer on its highest setting. Beat in
200 g sugar	
salt	Stir in in about 1 minute then whisk for a further 2 minutes. Sieve half of
200 g flour	over the eggs and fold in quickly on lowest setting. Fold in the remaining flour in the same way. Pour the mixture into a piping bag with a large nozzle and pipe puffs about 2 cm thick on to greased, floured baking sheets. Sprinkle with
75 g peeled chopped almonds	and bake in the oven.
Electricity:	
Conventional	200 (preheated)
Convection	About 170 (preheated)
Gas:	3 – 4 (preheated)
Baking time:	About 10 minutes
	Remove the biscuits from the baking sheets as soon as they come out of the oven.
	For the filling, melt
200 chocolate and hazel nut spread	in a small bowl in a water bath over a low heat, stirring until it is smooth. Spread the undersides of half the biscuits with the chocolate and hazelnut spread and sandwich together with the remaining biscuits. Melt
30-40 g chocolate glaze	in a small bowl in a water bath over a low heat, stirring until it is smooth. Sprinkle over the biscuits.
Packing suggestion if your want to give the chocolates as a gift:	Layer the biscuits in a decorative biscuit tin with aluminium foil between each layer. Close the tin. Gift wrap.

Carrot and nut cake

(wholefood cake)

	For the mixture, peel, wash and grate
500 g carrots	Mix together
500 g ground hazel nuts	
4 level tsp baking powder	Beat
8 egg yolks	
3 tbs orange juice	
grated peel of 1 orange (untreated)	and half of
300 g honey	to a thick cream using an electric mixer on its highest setting. Stiffly whisk
8 egg-whites	and fold them gradually into the cream, followed by the hazel nuts and, finally, the carrots. Pour the mixture into a springform baking pan (28 cm diameter, base greased and lined with greaseproof paper), put the baking pan on the wire shelf in the oven and bake.
Electricity:	
Conventional	175 – 200 (preheated)
Convection	150 – 160 (cold)
Gas:	3 – 4 (cold)
Baking time:	55 – 60 minutes
	Turn the cake out of the baking pan and leave to cool.
	For the apricot glaze push
2 tbs peach-apricot-maracuja-jam (prepared with pear juice thickening)	through a sieve and bring to the boil with
2 tbs water	stirring continuously. Brush the cake with this mixture.
	For the glaze, melt
150 g plain chocolate	
a little coconut fat	in a small bowl in a water bath over a low heat until smooth. Use to glaze the cake. Decorate with
marzipan carrots	if liked
Accompaniment:	Lightly sweetened, stiffly whipped cream.

Bismarck log

	For the sponge mixture, whisk
4 eggs,	
3–4 tbs hot water	for about 1 minute, until fluffy, using an electric mixer on its highest setting. Mix together
125 g sugar	
1 pkt vanilla sugar	Stir in in about 1 minute then whisk for a further 2 minutes. Mix together
75 g flour	
50 g cornflour	
1 pinch baking powder	Sieve half of the flour over the eggs and fold in quickly on lowest setting. Fold in the remaining flour in the same way. Spread the mixture about 1 cm thick on a greased baking sheet lined with greaseproof paper, putting a pleat in the paper at the open end of the baking sheet to make an edge, put the baking sheet in the oven and bake.
Electricity:	200–225 (preheated)
Gas:	3–4 (preheated)
Baking time:	10–15 minutes
	When baked, immediately turn the cake on to a kitchen towel sprinkled with sugar, brush the greaseproof paper with cold water and remove. Roll up the cake with the aid of the kitchen towel, leave to cool.
	For the filling, prepare a pudding from
1 pkt chocolate-flavoured pudding powder	
75–100 g sugar	
500 ml (½ l) milk	following the instructions on the packet. Leave to cool, stirring occasionally. Beat
200 g butter	until creamy, add the pudding by the spoonful (neither butter not pudding should be too cold as this would cause curdling). Carefully unroll the sponge roll and spread with some of the butter cream (reserving some for the outside). Roll up again. Remove the brown outer skin, spread the roll first thinly and then thickly with the remaining butter cream. Using a fork, decorate the cake with wavy lines to make it look like a log.

Sponge cake mixtures

Swiss roll
(photo p. 113)

	For the sponge mixture, whisk
3 eggs	
5–6 tbs hot water	for about 1 minute, until fluffy, using an electric mixer on its highest setting. Mix together
150 g sugar	
1 pkt vanilla sugar	Stir in in about 1 minute then whisk for a further 2 minutes. Mix together
100 g flour	
50 g cornflour	
1 level tsp baking powder	Sieve half of the flour over the eggs and fold in quickly on lowest setting. Fold in the remaining flour in the same way. Spread the mixture about 1 cm thick on a greased baking sheet (photo 1) lined with greaseproof paper, putting a pleat in the paper at the open end of the baking sheet to make an edge, put the baking sheet in the oven and bake.
Electricity:	200–225 (preheated)
Gas:	3–4 (preheated)
Baking time:	10–15 minutes When baked, immediately turn the cake on to a kitchen towel sprinkled with
sugar	Brush the greaseproof paper with cold water and remove quickly and carefully. Immediately spread the cake evenly with
250–375 g jam	(photo 2). Roll up the cake with the aid of the kitchen towel, starting at the narrow end (photo 3). Dust with
icing sugar	

Lightning cheesecake

	For the pastry, put
120 g sponge fingers	in a plastic bag and crush them with a rolling pin. Pour into a mixing bowl. Melt
75 g butter	Pour over the crumbs and stir. Spread the mixture evenly over the base of a springform baking pan (26 cm diameter, base greased) and press down firmly.
	For the filling, prepare
1 pkt lemon-flavoured jelly	with
200 ml water	Leave to stand for 10 minutes to swell. Heat, stirring continuously until the jelly has melted. Leave to cool off a little. Mix together
200 g double cream cheese	
125 g sugar	
1 pkt vanilla sugar	
2 tbs lemon juice	Stir in the lukewarm jelly and when the mixture starts to thicken, fold in
500 g (2 pots) stiffly whipped cream	Spread the mixture evenly over the pastry base and smooth the surface.
	For the topping, crumble
60 g sponge fingers	and sprinkle over the cheesecake. Refrigerate the cake until ready to serve.

Butter cream gateau

	For the sponge mixture, whisk
3 eggs,	
3-4 tbs hot water	for about 1 minute, until fluffy, using an electric mixer on its highest setting. Mix together
150 g sugar	
1 pkt vanilla sugar	Stir in in about 1 minute then whisk for a further 2 minutes. Mix together
100 g flour	
100 g cornflour	
3 level tsp baking powder	Sieve half of the flour over the eggs and fold in quickly on lowest setting. Fold in the remaining

	flour in the same way.
or	whisk
4 eggs	
2 tbs hot water	for about 1 minute, until fluffy, using an electric mixer on its highest setting. Mix together
150 g sugar	
1 pkt vanilla sugar	Stir in in about 1 minute then whisk for a further 2 minutes. Mix together
100 g flour	
100 g cornflour	
2 level tsps baking powder	Sieve half of the flour over the eggs and fold in quickly on lowest setting. Fold in the remaining flour in the same way. Pour the mixture into a springform baking pan (28 cm diameter, base greased and lined with greaseproof paper), put the baking pan on the wire shelf in the oven and bake.
Electricity:	175 – 200 (preheated)
Gas:	3 – 4 (cold)
Baking time:	20 – 30 minutes
	Remove the sponge from the springform pan and leave to cool
	For a chocolate butter cream, prepare a pudding from
1 pkt chocolate-flavoured pudding powder	
25 g sugar	
500 ml (½ l) milk	following the instructions on the packet but using only 25 g sugar. Break
100 g plain chocolate	into small pieces and add to the hot pudding, stirring until it has melted. Leave to cool, stirring occasionally
or	for a pale butter cream, prepare a pudding from
1 pkt vanilla, almond, cream or caramel-flavoured pudding powder	
75 – 100 g sugar	
500 ml (½ l) milk	following the instructions on the packet but using only 75 – 100 g sugar. Leave to cool, stirring occasionally
or	for a coffee butter cream, prepare a pudding from
1 pkt chocolate-flavoured pudding powder	
75 – 100 g sugar	
1 tbs instant coffee powder	
500 ml (½ l) milk	following the instructions on the packet but using only 75 – 100 g sugar. Leave to cool, stirring occasionally.

Sponge cake mixtures

	Beat
250 g butter	until creamy, add the pudding by the spoonful (neither butter not pudding should be too cold as this would cause curdling). Slice the sponge cake through twice and spread ¼ of the butter cream on the bottom layer (if preferred the sponge layer can first be brushed with 2 – 3 tbs jam). Put the second layer on top and spread with half the remaining cream. Cover with the third layer. Thinly spread the top and sides of the cake with the remaining butter cream and sprinkle the sides with
chocolate flakes or	
peeled, chopped, toasted almonds	Decorate with the remaining butter cream.

Walnut and chocolate cake

	For the kneaded pastry, mix together
125 g flour	
1 level tsp baking powder	
10 g cocoa	Sieve into a mixing bowl and add
50 g sugar	
75 g soft butter or margarine	Using the kneading attachment on the mixer, knead the ingredients on a low setting, switching to high. Remove from the mixing bowl and knead on the work surface until you have a smooth ball. Refrigerate for a while. Roll the pastry out thinly and use it to line a springform pan (28 cm diameter, base greased). Prick several times with a fork and bake in the spring form pan on the wire shelf in the oven.
Electricity:	
Conventional	200 – 225 (preheated)
Convection	170 (preheated)
Gas:	3 – 4 (preheated)
Baking time:	About 15 minutes When baking is finished, loosen the pastry from the base of the springform pan, allow to cool then transfer to a cake stand.

	For the sponge mixture, whisk
4 eggs	
3 – 4 tbs hot water	for about 1 minute, until fluffy, using an electric mixer on its highest setting. Mix together
100 g sugar	
1 pkt vanilla sugar	Stir in in about 1 minute then whisk for a further 2 minutes. Mix together
50 g flour	
1 level tsp baking powder	Sieve the flour over the eggs and fold in quickly on lowest setting. In the same way fold in
100 g ground walnuts	Spread the mixture on a baking sheet, greased and lined with greaseproof paper, folding the paper into a pleat to form an edge at the open side of the baking sheet, push into the oven and bake.
Electricity:	200 – 250 (preheated)
Gas:	3 – 4 (preheated)
Baking time:	12 – 15 minutes
	Turn the cake out on to a clean kitchen towel sprinkled with
sugar	Brush the greaseproof paper with cold water and pull off quickly but carefully.
	For the filling, prepare a pudding from
1 pkt vanilla-flavoured pudding powder	
50 g sugar	
500 ml (½ l) milk	following the instructions on the packet. Cream
250 g soft butter	Stir in the pudding by the spoonful. Break
100 g plain chocolate	into small pieces and add to the hot pudding, stirring until it has melted. Mix with half the butter cream. Spread the chocolate cream on the sponge cake and cut this into strips about 4 cm wide. Brush the pastry base with
2 – 3 tbs apricot jam	Place the sponge strips on the pastry base in a spiral pattern. Stir
2 – 3 tbs rum	into the remaining butter cream. Remove 2 – 3 tbs of the cream into a piping bag with a smooth nozzle. Spread the cake with the remaining cream and decorate it with the cream in the piping bag. Garnish with
walnut halves	

Coffee cream gateau

(photo p. 119)

	For the mixture, whisk
2 eggs	
2 – 3 tbs hot water	for about 1 minute, until fluffy, using an electric mixer on its highest setting. Mix together
100 g sugar	
1 pkt vanilla sugar	Stir in in about 1 minute then whisk for a further 2 minutes. Mix together
75 g flour	
50 g cornflour	
1 level tsp baking powder	Sieve half the flour over the eggs and fold in quickly on lowest setting. Fold in the remaining flour in the same way. Pour the mixture into a springform baking pan (28 cm diameter, base greased and lined with greaseproof paper) and push into the oven on the wire shelf.
Electricity:	175 – 200 (preheated)
Gas:	3 – 4 (cold)
Baking time:	20 – 30 minutes
	Remove from the springform pan and allow to cool.
	For the filling, dissolve
2 slightly rounded tsp instant coffee powder	in 2 tbs cream taken from
750 g (3 pots) double cream	Beat the remaining cream for ½ minute. Sieve
50 g icing sugar	Mix with
1 pkt vanilla sugar	
3 pkts cream stiffener	Sprinkle into the cream and beat until stiff. Stir in the dissolved coffee. Slice through the sponge cake once, spread ⅔ of the coffee cream on the bottom layer, cover with the top layer, pressing it on firmly, spread the top and sides of the cake with most of the remaining cream, reserving some for decoration. Sprinkle the sides with
grated chocolate	Decorate with the reserved cream and
12 chocolate coffee beans	

Lemon cream roll

	For the mixture, whisk
4 eggs	
3–4 tbs hot water	for about 1 minute, until fluffy, using an electric mixer on its highest setting. Mix together
125 g sugar	
1 pkt vanilla sugar	Stir in in about 1 minute then whisk for a further 2 minutes. Mix together
75 g flour	
50 g cornflour	
pinch baking powder	Sieve the flour over the eggs and fold in quickly on lowest setting. Fold in the remaining flour in the same way. Spread the mixture on a baking sheet, greased and lined with greaseproof paper, folding the paper into a pleat to form an edge at the open side of the baking sheet, push into the oven and bake.
Electricity:	200–225 (preheated)
Gas:	3–4 (preheated)
Baking time:	10–15 minutes
	Turn the cake out on to a clean kitchen towel sprinkled with sugar. brush the greaseproof paper with cold water and pull off quickly but carefully. Roll up the sponge with the kitchen towel.
	For the filling, mix
2 level tsps white gelatine powder	
2 tbs cold water	in a small pan and leave to swell for 10 minutes. Rub the
yellow skin of ½ lemon (untreated)	with the corners of
3 sugar cubes	Add the sugar to the gelatine and heat, stirring continuously, until fully dissolved. Add
5 tbs lemon juice	Beat
500 g (2 pots) double cream	until almost stiff, gradually stir the gelatine solution into the cream. Continue beating until really stiff. Sieve and fold in
100 g icing sugar	Carefully unroll the sponge, spread with ⅔ of the lemon cream, roll up again, removing the outer brown skin.
	Spread the remaining cream on the roll, first thinly and then thickly. Using a fork, mark a wavy pattern in the cream.

Almond fingers

	For the mixture, whisk
6 egg whites	until almost stiff. Gradually beat in
250 g sugar	Mix together
60 g flour	
10 g cocoa	and carefully fold in to the mixture. On lowest setting, stir in
200 g unpeeled, ground almonds	Finally stir in
60 g melted, cooled butter	Pour the almond mixture into a piping bag with a smooth nozzle and pipe sets of three strips (3 – 4 cm long) close to each other on to a greased baking sheet lined with greaseproof paper. Push into the oven.
Electricity:	
Conventional	175 – 200 (preheated)
Convection	160 (preheated)
Gas:	3 – 4 (preheated)
Baking time:	About 12 minutes
	For the filling, heat
about 150 g chocolate and hazel nut spread	in a small bowl in a water bath on a low heat until soft, stirring continuously. Spread the flat surfaces of half the biscuits with this mixture and cover with the remaining biscuits to make sandwiches.
	For the glaze, melt
100 g dark glaze	in a small bowl in a water bath on a low heat. Dip the ends of the biscuits in the glaze, leave to dry on greaseproof paper. Store in airtight tins.

Orange biscuits

	For the mixture, whisk
2 eggs	
grated peel of one orange (untreated)	
2 tbs orange juice	for about 1 minute, until fluffy, using an electric mixer on its highest setting. Mix together
100 g sugar	
1 pkt vanilla sugar	Stir in in about 1 minute then whisk for a further 2 minutes. Mix together
100 g flour	
50 g cornflour	
1 pkt vanilla-flavoured pudding powder	Sieve the mixture over the eggs and quickly fold in half on lowest setting. Fold in the remainder in the same way. Using 2 teaspoons place small mounds of the mixture on a greased and floured baking sheet (not too close together), push into the oven and bake.
Electricity:	
Conventional	175 – 200 (preheated)
Convection	160 – 170 (preheated)
Gas:	3 – 4 (preheated)
Baking time:	About 10 minutes
	For the glaze, sieve
100 g icing sugar	and mix to a smooth paste with
2 tbs orange juice	Use to decorate the biscuits (with the aid of a teaspoon). Garnish with
candied orange pieces	

Chocolate cream gateau

	For the mixture, whisk
2 eggs	
2 – 3 tbs hot water	for about 1 minute, until fluffy, using an electric mixer on its highest setting. Mix together
100 g sugar	
1 pkt vanilla sugar	Stir in in about 1 minute then whisk for a further 2 minutes. Mix together

75 g flour	
50 g cornflour	
1 level tsp baking powder	Sieve the mixture over the eggs and fold in half quickly on lowest setting. Fold in the remainder in the same way. Pour the mixture into a springform pan (28 cm diameter, base greased and lined with greaseproof paper) on the wire shelf in the oven.
Electricity:	175 – 200 (preheated)
Gas:	3 – 4 (cold)
Baking time:	20-30 minutes Remove the cake from the springform pan and leave to cool.
	For the filling, break
175 g chocolate	into small pieces and melt in a small pan, stirring continuously until smooth. Leave to cool. Mix together
1 pkt white gelatine powder	
4 tbs cold water	in a small pan. Leave to swell for 10 minutes. Heat, stirring continuously, until dissolved. Beat
750 g (3 pots) double cream	until almost stiff, stir in the gelatine solution, continue beating until really stiff. Stir 2 tbs of cream into the melted chocolate, then stir the chocolate into the cream. Cut the cake through once and spread ⅔ of the cream on the bottom layer. Cover with the top layer, pressing it on firmly. Spread some of the remaining cream evenly over the top and sides of the cake, sprinkle the sides and top with
25 g grated chocolate	and decorate with the remaining cream and
chocolate shapes	

Redcurrant gateau

	For the kneaded pastry, sieve
150 g flour	into a mixing bowl, add
40 g sugar	
1 pkt vanilla sugar	
2 egg yolks	
75 g soft butter or margarine	

Continued on page 124

	Using the kneading attachment on the mixer, knead the ingredients on a low setting, switching to high. Remove from the mixing bowl and knead on the work surface until you have a smooth ball. If the pastry sticks, refrigerate it for a while. Roll the pastry out thinly and use it to line a springform pan (28 cm diameter, base greased). Prick several times with a fork and bake in the spring form pan on the wire shelf in the oven.
Electricity:	
Conventional	200 – 225 (preheated)
Convection	170 (preheated)
Gas:	3 – 4 (cold)
Baking time:	About 15 minutes When baking is finished loosen the pastry from the base of the springform pan, allow to cool.
	For the almond sponge mixture, whisk
2 egg-whites	until stiff. Beat in
2 heaped tbs sugar	
salt	Add
3 egg yolks	Sieve
2 heaped tbs flour	and fold in together with
2 tbs peeled, ground almonds	Spoon the mixture into a springform pan (28 cm diameter, base greased and lined with greaseproof paper) on the wire shelf in the oven.
Electricity:	
Conventional	175 – 200 (preheated)
Convection	160 – 170 (preheated)
Gas:	3 – 4 (cold)
Baking time:	About 15 minutes Remove the cake from the springform pan immediately and turn out on to a cake rack, Remove greaseproof paper and leave to cool.
	For the topping, wash drain and strip
1 kg redcurrants	Sprinkle with
175 g sugar	Leave to draw juice. Bring to the boil. Mix together
50-60 g cornflour	
5 tbs cold water	Use to thicken the redcurrants, allow to cool, stirring occasionally.

	Spread the short pastry base with
redcurrant jelly	Cover with the sponge cake. Spread on the redcurrant mixture (photo 1). Whisk
3 egg-whites	until stiff. Gradually beat in
150 g sugar	Spread half the egg-white mixture over the cake (photo 2). Put the remaining egg-white into a piping bag with a star shaped nozzle and use to decorate the cake. Put the cake into the oven and bake until the meringue topping is lightly browned.
Electricity:	225 – 250 (preheated)
Gas:	4 – 5 (preheated)
Baking time:	About 5 minutes
Accompaniment:	Stiffly whipped fresh cream

Hazel nut puffs

	Using an electric mixer on its highest setting, beat
3 egg-whites	until very stiff. A cut made in the mixture with a knife must remain visible. Gradually beat in
200 g sugar	Reserve 3-4 tbs of egg-white. Fold
pinch ground cinnamon	
200 g ground hazel nuts	into the remaining egg-white. Transfer the mixture to a piping bag and pipe puffs on to a greased baking sheet lined with greaseproof paper. Wash out the piping bag and put the reserved egg-white into it. Pipe a little on to each puff. Push one hazel nut taken from
100 g hazel nuts	into each puff and bake in the oven.
Electricity:	
Conventional	130 – 150 (preheated)
Convection	100 (preheated)
Gas:	1 – 2 (cold)
Baking time:	About 25 minutes

The puffs should still feel a little soft when you take them out of the oven.

Sponge cake mixtures

Flowered petits fours
(photo p. 127)

	For the mixture, whisk
4 eggs	for about 1 minute, until fluffy, using an electric mixer on its highest setting. Stir in
125 g sugar	
salt	in about 1 minute then whisk for a further 2 minutes. Sieve
125 g flour	over the eggs and fold in quickly on lowest setting. Carefully stir in
60 g melted, cooled butter	
or margarine	Pour the mixture into a low sided rectangular 30x24 cm baking pan (base greased and lined with greaseproof paper) and push into the oven on the wire shelf.
Electricity:	175–200 (preheated)
Gas:	2–3 (cold)
Baking time:	20–25 minutes
	Turn the sponge cake out on to a cake rack, remove greaseproof paper, allow to cool. Cut the cake into small squares (4x4 cm) and cut these in turn into three pieces.
	For the chocolate and hazel nut cream filling, melt
100 g chocolate and hazel nut spread	in a small bowl in a water bath over a low heat, stirring continuously. To make 1 petit four, spread 2 sponge squares with the cream and top with a third square. Continue until ⅓ of the sponge squares have been used up.
	For the marzipan filling, knead together
100 g almond paste	
1 pkt rum baking aroma	Roll out thinly, cut into small squares (4x4 cm). Layer the marzipan squares and sponge squares into petits fours. Continue until ⅔ of the sponge squares are used up.
	For the jam filling, push
100 g raspberry jam	through a sieve and heat. Stir in
2 tbs chopped pistachio nuts	To make 1 petit four, brush 2 sponge squares with jam, top with a third square, repeat until all the sponge is used up.

Continued on page 128

Sponge cake mixtures

	In a water bath, melt
1 bag of dark cake glaze	and use to cover the chocolate and hazel nut cream petits fours. Decorate with
green icing	
chocolate leaves	
	In a water bath, melt
2 bags lemon cake glaze	and use half to cover the marzipan cakes. Decorate with
red icing	
sugar flowers	Colour the remaining lemon glaze pink with
red food colouring	Use to cover the remaining petits fours. Decorate with
glace cherry halves	
chopped pistachio nuts	

Pineapple and brittle cream cake

	For the mixture, whisk
3 eggs	
3 – 4 tbs hot water	for about 1 minute, until fluffy, using an electric mixer on its highest setting. Mix together
150 g sugar	
1 pkt vanilla sugar	Stir in in about 1 minute then whisk for a further 2 minutes. Mix together
100 g flour	
100 g cornflour	
3 level tsps baking powder	Sieve half the flour over the eggs and fold in quickly on lowest setting. Fold in the remaining flour in the same way. Pour the mixture into a springform baking pan (28 cm diameter, base greased and lined with greaseproof paper) and push into the oven on the wire shelf.
Electricity:	175 – 200 (preheated)
Gas:	3 – 4 (cold)
Baking time:	20 – 30 minutes
	Remove from the springform pan, allow to cool and slice through twice.

	For the filling, prepare a pudding from
1 pkt vanilla-flavoured pudding powder	
500 ml (½ l) milk	
50 g sugar	following the instructions on the packet. Leave to cool stirring occasionally.
	For the brittle, heat
1 tbs butter	
60 g sugar	until the mixture is golden and the sugar has melted. Add
125 g peeled, chopped almonds	Heat, stirring continuously until the mixture has browned. Pour on to an oiled baking sheet. When cold, crush the brittle into small pieces. Cream
250 g soft butter	and stir in the vanilla pudding by the spoonful. Stir half the brittle into half the butter cream. Drain
500 g tinned pineapple	and chop into pieces. Reserve 16 pieces for decoration. Spread the bottom layer of sponge with
2 – 3 tbs pineapple or apricot jam	Cover with pineapple pieces, spread with a little of the brittle and cream mixture and cover with the middle sponge layer. Spread the sponge with the remaining brittle cream and cover with the top sponge layer. Cover with half the reserved butter cream and mark into 16 slices using a moistened knife. Decorate the cake with the remaining butter cream and the reserved pineapple pieces. Sprinkle the sides of the cake with brittle.
Tip:	1. Flavour the butter cream with 2 – 3 tbs rum or brandy
	2. Brush the pineapple reserved for decoration with dissolved gelatine (mix 1 tsp white gelatine powder with 2 – 3 tbs cold water, leave to swell for 10 minutes, dissolve).

Kneaded pastry

Preparations

When making pastry with an electric mixer it is important that the fat is soft (spreadable).

If dried fruit is to be used in a kneaded pastry, it must be prepared as follows:
a) pick over currants and raisins, removing stalks etc.
b) peel almonds by immersing them in boiling water for 2 – 3 minutes (take pan off heat). Drain, peel and chop.

Generally speaking it is not necessary to grease baking sheets and pans.
Fruit flan cases, tartlet cases and baking sheets on which watery or milky pastries are to be baked are the exception.

The individual steps

" Mix flour and baking powder and sieve into a mixing bowl..."
Mixing and sieving loosen up and aerate the flour and ensure that the baking powder is distributed evenly through it. This makes pastry lighter. If the recipe calls for cocoa, this should also be added to the flour.

When using wholemeal flour, mix the flour and baking powder in a mixing bowl.

"Add the remaining ingredients shown in the recipe..."
Always break eggs one at a time into a cup first to check that they are good. If the recipe specifies any liquid this should be added on top of the sugar or honey.
Fat (margarine or butter) must be soft (spreadable). The ingredients will only combine well if the above instructions are followed. If more flour is added to a high-fat pastry than is specified in the recipe, the pastry will be crumbly and hard. Any fruit must be kneaded in last.

..."First mix the ingredients on the lowest mixer setting for a moment before switching to high and combining them thoroughly..."
The ingredients will mix best if the fat is soft (spreadable). It is therefore important to take the fat out of the refrigerator in plenty of time.

..."Turn the pastry out on to the floured work surface and knead to a smooth ball by hand..."
Do not put too much flour on the work surface, otherwise the pastry will break. Knead the pastry quickly keeping your fingers together and your hands flat.

Kneaded pastry

..."Shape this into a roll.

If the pastry sticks, pop it into the refrigerator for a while, or add a little extra flour."
The pastry will be easier to roll out if it is shaped into a roll. Refrigerating high-fat pastry makes it less likely to stick. If pastries with a high water or milk content stick, a little extra flour may be added to them.
Make sure no bits of pastry are left sticking to the work surface before rolling out the pastry as this is another cause of sticking. The work surface should be sprinkled evenly with flour.

Rolling out pastry
To preserve the texture of the pastry it is advisable to roll out small pieces (this applies especially for biscuits). The rolling pin must actually roll lightly across the pastry, not crushing it.
In between rolling, occasionally run a long knife between the pastry and the work surface. This will loosen it at once if it starts to stick anywhere.

When making biscuits cut out the shapes in a way which makes the best possible use of the pastry. Rekneading, rolling and cutting do not improve the texture of the pastry.

Kneaded pastry for fruit flans should be baked in springform baking pans or in greased flan baking pans. If using a springform pan, line the base with ⅔ of the specified amount of pastry. Shape the remaining pastry (depending on the recipe) into a roll and place it around the edge of the pastry base, pressing it on and up with two fingers to make an edge about 3 cm high. Prick the base several times with a fork to avoid blistering.

Baking kneaded pastry.

All kneaded pastry should be baked as directed in the recipe. Remove the pastry from the baking pan or sheet as soon as it comes out of the oven and transfer it to a wire cake rack to cool off (put biscuits next to and not on top of each other).

Fruit flan
(wholefood cake)
(photo p. 130/131)

For the pastry, put

100 g finely milled wheat
100 g finely milled buckwheat
salt

into a mixing bowl. Mix together and add

1 tbs honey
100 g sour cream
100 g soft butter

Mix the ingredients for a moment, using the kneading attachment on the electric mixer and a low setting, then switch to high and knead thoroughly. Turn out on to the work surface and continue kneading by hand until you have a smooth ball of pastry. If it is a little sticky, pop it into the refrigerator for a while. Roll out the pastry a little larger than the base of a 28 cm diameter springform baking pan and use to line the

Kneaded pastry

greased base of the baking pan. Push the pastry up to make an edge about 2 cm high. Prick the pastry several times with a fork, bake on the wire shelf in the oven.

Electricity:
Conventional 175 – 200 (preheated)
Convection 160 – 170 (cold)
Gas: 3 – 4 (cold)
Baking time: 20 – 25 minutes

For the filling, arrange
600 – 700 g berries (e.g. strawberries, raspberries, blackberries) or stewed apricots
in the cold flan case. Heat
3 heaped tbs jam (appropriate to the fruit you have used)
in a pan, stirring continuously and brush over the fruit.

Friesian Christmas cake
(photo p. 137)

For the pastry, mix
250 g flour
pinch of baking powder
2 pkts vanilla sugar
and sieve into a mixing bowl. Add
1 pot (150 g) crème fraîche
175 g soft butter
Mix the ingredients for a moment, using the kneading attachment on the electric mixer and a low setting, then switch to high and knead thoroughly. Turn out on to the work surface and continue kneading by hand until you have a smooth ball of pastry.

Continued on page 138

	If it is a little sticky, pop it into the refrigerator for a while. Divide the pastry into 4 equal pieces and roll out each piece to fit the greased base of a 28 cm diameter springform baking pan (make sure the pastry is not too thin at the edges). Prick the pastry several times with a fork (photo 1). Fit the springform ring.
	For the crumble, sieve
150 g flour	into a mixing bowl and mix with
75 g sugar	
1 pkt vanilla sugar	
pinch ground cinnamon	Add
100 g soft butter	and mix with the kneading attachment on the mixer until the mixture turns into crumbs. Sprinkle the pastry layers evenly with the crumble and bake on the wire shelf in the oven.
Electricity:	
Conventional	200 – 225 (preheated)
Convection	170 – 180 (preheated)
Gas:	3 – 4 (preheated)
Baking time:	About 15 minutes
	Remove the pastry from the springform bases as soon as they come out of the oven and cut one of the pastry layers into 12 slices (photo 2). Leave on a cake rack to cool off.
	For the filling, beat
500 g (2 pots) double cream	for ½ minute. Sprinkle in
25 g sugar	
2 pkts cream stiffener	
1 pkt vanilla sugar	Beat until stiff. Transfer the cream to a piping bag with a serrated nozzle.
	Spread each of the 3 whole layers with ⅓ of
450 g plum preserve	Pipe the cream on top (photo 3). Layer to form a cake, finishing with the sliced pastry layer. Sprinkle with
icing sugar snow	Store the cake in the refrigerator until needed. Cut slices with a bread knife before serving.
Tip:	Confectioners snow can be used instead of icing sugar. This does not need to be sieved and is not so easily absorbed by the pastry. (Available in ready to use packs).

Viennese apple strudel

	For the pastry, sieve
200 g flour	on to the work surface, make a depression in the centre and sprinkle in a little
salt	Slowly add
5 large tbs lukewarm water	
50 g melted butter or margarine or	
3 tbs cooking oil	and mix to a thick paste with some of the flour. Working from the centre, quickly knead all the ingredients to a smooth dough. Place the ball of dough on greaseproof paper inside a hot, dry pan (boil water in it beforehand) cover with a lid and leave to rest for 30 minutes.
	For the filling, peel, quarter, core and finely chop
1 – 1 ½ kg apples	Mix with
½ phial rum flavouring	
3 drops lemon-flavoured baking oil	Sort
50 g raisins	Melt
75 g butter or margarine	Roll out the strudel pastry on a large, floured cloth (table cloth). Brush thinly with a little of the fat. Using your hands, carefully pull the pastry until you have a rectangle 50 x 70 cm. It must be transparent. If the edges are thicker, cut them off. Brush the pastry with ⅔ of the fat. Sprinkle
50 g breadcrumbs	on the pastry (except for 3 cm at each of the short sides). Distribute the apple, raisins
100 g sugar	
1 pkt vanilla sugar	
50 g peeled, chopped almonds	over the pastry. Fold the uncovered pastry ends over the filling. Roll up the pastry from one of the long sides. Press the edges together firmly. Place on a greased baking sheet, brush with fat and bake.
Electricity:	
Conventional	175 – 200(preheated)
Convection	160 – 170 (cold)
Gas:	3 4 (preheated)
Baking time:	45 – 55 minutes Brush the strudel with the remaining butter during baking.

Kneaded pastry

Quark and poppyseed cake
(photo p. 141)

	For the pastry, mix
500 g flour	
2 level tsp baking powder	and sieve into a mixing bowl. Add
125 g sugar	
1 pkt vanilla sugar	
2 eggs	
250 g soft butter or margarine	
	Mix the ingredients for a moment, using the kneading attachment on the electric mixer and a low setting, then switch to high and knead thoroughly. Turn out on to the work surface and continue kneading by hand until you have a smooth ball of pastry. If the pastry sticks pop it into the refrigerator for a while.
	For the poppyseed filling, bring to the boil
500 ml (½ l) milk	Remove from heat and stir in
375 g freshly ground poppyseeds	Leave to swell. As soon as the mixture has cooled off a little, stir in
75-100 g sugar	
2 tbs honey, 2 eggs	
100 g sultanas	
50 g breadcrumbs	Leave to cool off completely.
	For the quark filling, mix together
1 kg low fat quark	
200 g sugar	
2 eggs	
salt	
grated peel of ½ lemon (untreated)	
75 g melted butter	
1 pkt cheesecake stiffener	Roll out ⅔ of the pastry on to a greased baking sheet. Spread with the quark mixture. Distribute the poppyseed mixture over this. Roll out the remaining pastry and cut into 1 cm wide strips. Lay the pastry strips across the top of the cake in a criss cross pattern. Push the baking sheet into the oven and bake.

Continued on page 142

Kneaded pastry

Electricity:	
Conventional	175 – 200 (preheated)
Convection	160 – 170 (cold)
Gas:	3 – 4 (preheated)
Baking time:	About 50 minutes
	For the glaze, press
3 – 4 tbs apricot jam	through a sieve, mix with
3 tbs water	Bring to the boil and allow to boil until slightly thickened. Use to brush the surface of the cake.

Linzer slices

	For the pastry, mix
500 g flour	
½ pkt baking powder	
1 ½ – 2 tbs cocoa	and sieve into a mixing bowl. Add
300 g sugar	
1 egg	
1 egg-white	
1 phial rum flavouring	
1 phial arrak flavouring	
6 drops bitter almond baking oil	
grated peel of ½ lemon (untreated)	
2 – 3 tsp ground cinnamon	
2 pinches ground cloves	
300 g soft butter	
300 g ground hazel nuts	Mix the ingredients for a moment, using the kneading attachment on the electric mixer and a low setting, then switch to high and knead thoroughly. Turn out on to the work surface and continue kneading by hand until you have a smooth ball of pastry. Refrigerate for several hours. Roll out a good half of the pastry on to a greased baking sheet. Cover half with a thick layer of
thick plum preserve	and the other half with
raspberry and redcurrant jam	Roll out portions of the remaining pastry about 3 mm thick and cut into 1 cm strips. Use the strips to make a criss cross pattern on top of the cake.

	Beat together
1 egg yolk	
½ tbs milk	Use to brush the pastry on top of the cake. Push the baking sheet into the oven and bake.
Electricity:	
Conventional	200 (preheated)
Convection	170 (cold)
Gas:	3 – 4 (preheated)
Baking time:	25 – 30 minutes When cold cut the cake into slices.
Tip:	Linzer slices will keep for up to 3 weeks, stored in layers in an airtight tin.

Almond biscuits
(wholefood biscuits)

	Finely grind
300 g wheat	
75 g buckwheat	Put into a mixing bowl with
1 level tsp baking powder	
75 g cane sugar syrup	
seeds scraped from 1 vanilla pod	
sea salt	
1 egg yolk	
250 g soft butter	Mix the ingredients for a moment, using the kneading attachment on the electric mixer and a low setting, then switch to high and knead thoroughly. Quickly knead in
200 g whole, unpeeled almonds	Turn out on to the work surface and continue kneading by hand until you have a smooth ball of pastry. Shape the pastry into rolls 2 ½ to 3 cm in diameter and refrigerate until they are hard. Using a sharp knife cut the rolls into ½ cm thick slices, arrange on a greased baking sheet and bake in the oven.
Electricity:	
Conventional	175 – 200 (preheated)
Convection	160 – 170 (preheated)
Gas:	3 – 4 (preheated)
Baking time:	12 – 15 minutes

Florentine slices

	For the pastry, mix
200 g flour	
½ level tsp baking powder	and sieve into a mixing bowl. Add
75 g sugar	
1 pkt vanilla sugar	
2 tbs water	
100 g soft butter	Mix the ingredients for a moment, using the kneading attachment on the electric mixer and a low setting, then switch to high and knead thoroughly. Turn out on to the work surface and continue kneading by hand until you have a smooth ball of pastry. If the pastry sticks pop it into the refrigerator for a while. Roll out the pastry into a rectangle about 28x36 cm, cut in half so that you have two 14x36 cm pieces. Fold over 1 – 2 cm pastry along the long sides. Place the pastry strips on a greased baking sheet and bake.
Electricity:	
Conventional	200 (preheated)
Convection	170 (preheated)
Gas:	3 – 4 (preheated)
Baking time:	About 10 minutes
	For the filling, melt
50 g butter	Add
100 g sugar	
1 pkt vanilla sugar	
2 tbs honey	Allow to caramelize, stirring continuously. Pour on
250 g (1 pot) double cream	Keep stirring until the caramel mixture comes away from the pan. Add
100 g peeled, chopped almonds	
100 g chopped hazel nuts	
25 g chopped glace cherries	and keep stirring until the mixture thickens. Spread the mixture over the pastry strips, leaving the edges free, push into the oven and bake as above.
Baking time:	10 – 12 minutes.

	Leave to cool for a while before slicing into 2 – 3 cm wide strips. Melt
about 75 g chocolate glaze	in a small bowl in a water bath over low heat, stirring continuously until smooth. Use to coat the underside and the edges of the Florentine slices

Linzer cake

	For the pastry, mix
200 g flour	
1 level tsp baking powder	and sieve into a mixing bowl. Add
125 g sugar	
1 pkt vanilla sugar	
2 drops bitter almond baking oil	
pinch ground cloves	
1 level tsp ground cinnamon	
salt	
½ egg yolk	
1 egg-white	
125 g soft butter	
125 unpeeled, ground almonds	Mix the ingredients for a moment, using the kneading attachment on the electric mixer and a low setting, then switch to high and knead thoroughly. Turn out on to the work surface and continue kneading by hand until you have a smooth ball of pastry. Roll out half of the pastry to a sheet the size of a 26 cm diameter springform baking pan. Cut into 16 – 20 strips. Roll out the remaining pastry and use it to line the springform pan base. Spread with
100 g raspberry jam	leaving about 1 cm free of jam around the edge. Arrange the pastry strips over the jam in a criss cross pattern. Mix together
½ egg yolk	
1 tsp milk	Use to brush the pastry on top of the cake. Push the baking sheet into the oven and bake.
Electricity:	
Conventional	175 – 200 (preheated)
Convection	170 (cold)
Gas:	3 – 4 (cold)
Baking time:	25 – 30 minutes

Cinnamon leaves

(photo p. 147)

	For the pastry, sieve
300 g flour	into a mixing bowl. Add
75 g sugar	
1 heaped tsp ground cinnamon	
salt	
1 egg	
150 g soft butter	Mix the ingredients for a moment, using the kneading attachment on the electric mixer and a low setting, then switch to high and knead thoroughly. Turn out on to the work surface and continue kneading by hand until you have a smooth ball of pastry. If the pastry sticks pop it into the refrigerator for a while. Roll the pastry out thinly, cut out oval shapes and arrange these on a greased baking sheet lined with greaseproof paper. Beat together
1 egg yolk	
1 tbs milk	and brush the biscuits with this mixture. Sprinkle with a mixture of
cinnamon and sugar	Push the baking sheet into the oven and bake.
Electricity:	
Conventional	175 – 200 (preheated)
Convection	160 – 170 (preheated)
Gas:	3 – 4 (preheated)
Baking time:	12 – 15 minutes
	For the glaze, melt
40 – 50 g fat glaze	
40 – 50 g plain cooking chocolate	in a small bowl in a water bath over a low heat, stirring continuously until smooth. Brush the undersides of the biscuits with this mixture.

Kneaded pastry

Cheesecake

	For the pastry, sieve
150 g flour	into a mixing bowl. Add
40 g sugar	
1 pkt vanilla sugar	
100 g soft butter	Mix the ingredients for a moment, using the kneading attachment on the electric mixer and a low setting, then switch to high and knead thoroughly. Turn out on to the work surface and continue kneading by hand until you have a smooth ball of pastry. If the pastry sticks pop it into the refrigerator for a while. Roll out the pastry on the greased base of a springform baking pan (28 cm diameter). Line the springform ring with a strip of greaseproof paper and fit it to the base.
	For the filling, cream
250 g soft butter	Gradually add
200 g sugar	
1 pkt vanilla sugar	
7 egg yolks, salt	
grated peel of 1 lemon (untreated)	
3 tbs lemon juice	Slowly stir in
1 kg low fat quark	
1 pkt cheesecake stiffener	Whisk
7 egg-whites	until stiff and fold in. Distribute the mixture over the pastry base in the springform pan, smooth the surface and put on the wire shelf in the oven.
Electricity:	
Conventional	160 – 175 (preheated)
Gas:	2 (preheated)
Baking time:	70 – 80 minutes Leave the finished cake to stand in the oven for a further 30 – 45 minutes, leaving the oven door slightly ajar and the oven switched off. Remove and leave to cool off in the baking pan.

Apple crumble cake

	For the pastry, sieve
150 g flour	
pinch baking powder	into a mixing bowl. Add

Kneaded pastry

100 g sugar 1 pkt vanilla sugar salt, 1 egg 100 g soft butter	Mix the ingredients for a moment, using the kneading attachment on the electric mixer and a low setting, then switch to high and knead thoroughly. Turn out on to the work surface and continue kneading by hand until you have a smooth ball of pastry. If the pastry sticks pop it into the refrigerator for a while. Roll out ⅔ of the pastry on a greased springform baking pan base (28 cm diameter), prick several times with a fork, fit springform ring and bake on the wire shelf in the oven.
Electricity:	
Conventional	200 – 225 (preheated)
Convection	180 (preheated)
Gas:	3 – 4 (preheated)
Baking time:	10 – 12 minutes Leave the pastry to cool off. Shape the remaining pastry into a roll and fit it around the pastry base to form an edge. Press against the sides of the baking pan until you have an edge about 2 cm high.
	For the filling, peel, quarter, core and chop
about 1 ½ kg apples	Stew lightly together with
75 g sugar pinch ground cinnamon 75 g butter	stirring frequently. Leave to cool and spread over the baked pastry base.
	For the crumble, sieve
150 g flour	into a mixing bowl, add
100 g sugar 1 pkt vanilla sugar 100 g soft butter	and mix with the kneading attachment on the electric mixer until crumbs form. Spread these evenly over the apple and return the baking pan to the oven.
Electricity:	
Conventional	200 – 225 (preheated)
Convection	180 (cold)
Gas:	3 – 4 (cold)
Baking time:	About 40 minutes

French-style fruit flan

	For the pastry, sieve
200 g flour	into a mixing bowl. Add
1 pkt vanilla sugar	
salt, 1 egg	
100 g soft butter	Mix the ingredients for a moment, using the kneading attachment on the electric mixer and a low setting, then switch to high and knead thoroughly. Turn out on to the work surface and continue kneading by hand until you have a smooth ball of pastry. Refrigerate for a while. Roll out the pastry on a floured kitchen towel (photo 1) and use to line a greased flan dish (26 cm diameter).
	For the filling, wash, stone and cut in half
250 g apricots	Peel, quarter, core and slice
3 medium sized apples	
2 pears	Arrange the fruit on the in the flan dish (photo 2).
	For the glaze, beat together
2 egg yolks	
250 g (1 pot) double cream	Stir in
60 g sugar	
1 pkt vanilla sugar	
2 level tbs cornflour	Pour this mixture over the fruit (photo 2). Put the flan dish on the wire shelf in the oven.
Electricity:	
Conventional	175 – 200 (preheated)
Convection	160 – 170 (cold)
Gas:	3 – 4 (preheated)
Baking time:	About 50 minutes
	Push
4 – 5 tbs apricot jam	through a sieve, bring to the boil and use to glaze the flan as soon as it comes out of the oven (photo 4).

Kneaded pastry

Vanilla biscuits

	For the pastry, sieve
250 g flour	
pinch baking powder	into a mixing bowl. Add
125 g sugar	
1 pkt vanilla sugar	
3 egg yolks	
200 g soft butter	
125 g peeled ground almonds	Mix the ingredients for a moment, using the kneading attachment on the electric mixer and a low setting, then switch to high and knead thoroughly. Turn out on to the work surface and continue kneading by hand until you have a smooth ball of pastry. If the pastry sticks pop it into the refrigerator for a while. Shape the pastry into rolls as thick as your thumb, cut off 2 cm lengths, shape these into rolls 5 cm long with the ends thinner than the middle. Make crescent shapes and arrange on a baking sheet.
Electricity:	
Conventional	175 – 200 (preheated)
Convection	160 – 170 (preheated)
Gas:	3 – 4 (preheated)
Baking time:	10 – 15 minutes
	Sieve
50 g icing sugar	Mix with
1 pkt vanilla sugar	and turn the biscuits in this mixture while they are still hot.

Fruit flan

	For the pastry, sieve
150 g flour	
½ level tsp baking powder	into a mixing bowl. Add
75 g sugar	
1 pkt vanilla sugar	
salt, 1 egg	
75 g soft butter or margarine	Mix the ingredients for a moment, using the kneading attachment on the electric mixer and a low setting, then switch to high and knead thoroughly. Turn out on to the work surface and continue kneading by hand until you have a smooth ball of pastry.

Kneaded pastry

	If the pastry sticks pop it into the refrigerator for a while. Roll out ⅔ of the pastry on to the greased 28 cm diameter base of a springform baking pan. Knead
1 level tbs flour	into the remaining pastry, shape it into a roll and fit it around the pastry base to form an edge. Press against the sides of the baking pan until you have an edge about 2 cm high. Prick the base several times with a fork and put the baking pan on the wire shelf in the oven.
Electricity:	
Conventional	200 – 225 (preheated)
Convection	170 – 180 (cold)
Gas:	3 – 4 (preheated)
Baking time:	15 – 20 minutes
	When the flan has cooled off sprinkle cream stiffener over the base to stop it becoming soggy when covered with fruit.
	For the filling, wash, trim and drain (raspberries should only be picked over)
1 kg raw fruit (e.g. strawberries, raspberries, red or blackcurrants, bilberries, grapes)	Sprinkle with
sugar	and leave to stand for a while
or	drain
stewed or preserved fruit (e.g. apricots, peaches, sour cherries, gooseberries)	and arrange the fruit on the flan.
	For the glaze, prepare
1 pkt flan glaze	
sugar as instructed	
250 ml (¼ l) water or fruit juice	as directed on the packet. Pour over the fruit. Decorate the sides of the flan with
peeled, flaked almonds.	If your flan dish (28 cm diameter) has a serrated edge, roll out ⅔ of the pastry into a circle of 29 cm diameter, sprinkle the base of the dish with breadcrumbs, line with the pastry. Shape the remaining pastry into a roll, put it round the sides of the flan dish, pressing it firmly against the sides until you have a smooth surface. Prick the base several times with a fork.

Kneaded pastry

Milanese marzipan tartlets
(photo p. 155)

	For the pastry, sieve
200 g flour	into a mixing bowl. Add
65 g sugar	
grated peel of ½ lemon (untreated)	
125 g soft butter	Mix the ingredients for a moment, using the kneading attachment on the electric mixer and a low setting, then switch to high and knead thoroughly. Turn out on to the work surface and continue kneading by hand until you have a smooth ball of pastry. Refrigerate for a while. Roll out the pastry to a thickness of about 3 mm and stamp out round biscuits (photo 1) about 8 cm in diameter. Arrange the biscuits on a greased baking sheet lined with greaseproof paper.
	For the filling, cream
125 g almond paste	with the electric whisk, gradually add
30 g sieved icing sugar	
1 egg yolk	
1 tbs lemon juice	Keep beating until the mixture is creamy. Transfer to a piping bag with a small, serrated nozzle and pipe stars on to half the biscuits (photo 2). Push the baking sheet into the oven.
Electricity:	
Conventional	175 – 200 (preheated)
Convection	160 – 170 (preheated)
Gas:	3 – 4 (preheated)
Baking time:	About 15 minutes

Continued on page 156

Kneaded pastry

	For the filling, cream
75 g almond paste	with the electric whisk, stir in
1 – 2 tbs rum or arrak	
1 tbs apricot jam	Spread this on the plain biscuits and sandwich together with the decorated ones (photo 3). Quarter
3 – 4 glace cherries	and decorate each tartlet with a piece of cherry.
	For the apricot glaze, push
1 ½ tbs apricot jam	through a sieve, mix with
2 tbs water	Bring to the boil stirring continuously. Brush over the tartlets. If wished they can also be decorated with stiffly whipped cream.

Covered apple or cherry cake

	For the pastry, sieve
300 g flour	
2 level tsp baking powder	into a mixing bowl. Add
100 g sugar	
1 pkt vanilla sugar	
salt	
½ egg yolk	
1 egg-white	
1 tbs milk	
150 g soft butter or margarine	Mix the ingredients for a moment, using the kneading attachment on the electric mixer and a low setting, then switch to high and knead thoroughly. Turn out on to the work surface and continue kneading by hand until you have a smooth ball of pastry. If the pastry sticks pop it into the refrigerator for a while. Roll out half the pastry on to the greased base of a 28 cm diameter springform baking pan, prick several times with a fork, fit the springform ring and bake on the wire shelf in the oven.
Electricity:	
Conventional	200 – 225 (preheated)
Convection	170 – 180 (preheated)
Gas:	3 – 4 (preheated)
Baking time:	15 – 20 minutes

	For the apple filling, sort
50 g raisins	Peel, quarter, core and chop coarsely
about 2 kg apples	Stew lightly with the raisins and
1 tbs water	
30 g butter	
50 g sugar	
½ tsp ground cinnamon	Flavour with
50 g sugar	
a few drops of rum flavouring or lemon baking oil	
or	
	for the cherry filling, wash, drain, trim and stone
1 kg sour cherries	Mix with
100 g sugar	Leave to draw juice for a while. Bring to the boil briefly, drain. When the juice and the cherries are cold, measure 250 ml (¼ l) juice (make up with water if necessary). Mix 4 tbs of the juice with
20 g cornflour	Bring the remaining juice to the boil, stir in the cherries. Leave to cool completely. Sweeten with
1 tbs sugar.	Roll out the remaining pastry into a circle the size of the baking pan. Shape the leftover pastry into a roll and place it around the baked pastry base to form an edge, pressing it against the springform ring until the edge is about 3 cm high. Pour the filling into the pastry case, cover with the pastry top, prick several times with a fork or roll a criss cross pattern on to it with a pastry wheel. Put on the wire shelf in the oven.
Electricity:	
Conventional	200 – 225 (preheated)
Convection	170 (cold)
Gas:	3 – 4 (preheated)
Baking time:	20 – 30 minutes

Tip: Serve the apple or cherry cake covered with a thick topping of whipped cream. Add a little Kirsch or Calvados to the cream when beating it.

Quark envelopes

(photo p. 159)

	For the pastry, sieve
150 g flour	into a mixing bowl. Add
1 pkt vanilla sugar	
salt	
150 g low fat quark	
150 g soft butter	Mix the ingredients for a moment, using the kneading attachment on the electric mixer and a low setting, then switch to high and knead thoroughly. Turn out on to the work surface and continue kneading by hand until you have a smooth ball of pastry. Refrigerate for 1 hour.
	For the filling, mix together
250 g full fat quark	
50 g sugar	
1 pkt vanilla sugar	
1 egg-white	Stir in
30 g raisins	Roll out half the pastry into a 30x30 cm square and cut into 10x10 cm squares. Put a little of the filling into the centre of each square. Beat
1 egg yolk	
1 ½ tbs milk	and use to brush the edges of the pastry. Fold the pastry to form envelopes, and brush with the remaining egg. Repeat with the other half of the pastry. Roll out the left over pastry and cut into small strips. Put two diagonally crossed strips on each pastry envelope. Brush with egg and bake on the baking sheet.
Electricity:	
Conventional	200 – 225 (preheated)
Convection	180 (preheated)
Gas:	3 – 4 (preheated)
Baking time:	About 25 minutes

Orange and chocolate biscuits

	For the pastry, mix
200 g flour	
60 g cornflour	
1 level tsp baking powder	and sieve into a mixing bowl. Add
100 g sugar	
1 pkt vanilla sugar	
grated peel of 1 orange (untreated)	
1 egg	
125 g soft butter	Mix the ingredients for a moment, using the kneading attachment on the electric mixer and a low setting, then switch to high and knead thoroughly. Chop
100g plain chocolate	into small pieces, knead in briefly on medium setting. Turn out on to the work surface and continue kneading by hand until you have a smooth ball of pastry. Shape the pastry into 3 rolls, 3 cm in diameter, and press them flat to form strips about 5 cm wide and a good 1 cm high. Refrigerate until the pastry is hard. Cut the strips into slices ½ cm thick with a sharp knife. Arrange on a baking sheet and bake in the oven.
Electricity:	
Conventional	175 – 200 (preheated)
Convection	160 – 170 (preheated)
Gas:	3 – 4 (preheated)
Baking time:	About 10 minutes

Cherry and almond cake

	For the pastry, mix
150 g flour	
½ level tsp baking powder	and sieve into a mixing bowl. Add
50 g sugar	
1 pkt vanilla sugar	
1 egg-white	
100 g soft butter	Mix the ingredients for a moment, using the kneading attachment on the electric mixer and a low setting, then switch to high and knead thoroughly. Turn out on to the work surface and con-

tinue kneading by hand until you have a smooth ball of pastry. If the pastry sticks, pop it into the refrigerator for a while. Roll out ⅔ of the pastry on to the greased 28 cm diameter base of a springform baking pan.
Shape the remaining pastry into a roll and fit it around the pastry base to form an edge. Press against the sides of the baking pan until you have an edge about 1 – 2 cm high.
Prick the base several times with a fork and sprinkle with breadcrumbs.

	For the filling, drain
500 g stoned sour cherries (preserved)	and arrange on the pastry base. Mix together
1 egg yolk	
75 g sugar	
1 pkt vanilla sugar	
3 tbs double cream	
15 g cornflour	Stir in
100 g peeled, chopped almonds	Distribute this mixture over the cherries and put the baking pan on the wire shelf in the oven.
Electricity:	
Conventional	175 – 200 (preheated)
Convection	160 (cold)
Gas:	3 – 4 (cold)
Baking time:	About 45 minutes

Hazel nut ring

	For the pastry, mix
300 g flour	
2 level tsp baking powder	and sieve into a mixing bowl. Add
100 g sugar	
1 pkt vanilla sugar	
salt	
1 egg	
2 tbs milk or water	
125 g soft butter or margarine	Mix the ingredients for a moment, using the kneading attachment on the electric mixer and a low setting, then switch to high and knead thoroughly. Turn out on to the work surface and continue kneading by hand until you have a smooth ball of pastry. If the pastry sticks pop it into the refrigerator for a while.

Kneaded pastry

	For the filling, mix together
200 g ground hazel nuts	
100 g sugar	
4–5 drops bitter almond baking oil	
½ egg yolk	
1 egg-white	
3–4 tbs water	until you have a smooth paste. Roll the pastry into a rectangle 35x45 cm, spread with the nut paste, then roll up, starting at one of the long sides. Shape into a ring and put on a greased baking sheet. Beat
½ egg yolk	
1 tbs milk	Brush the ring with the egg, make cuts across the pastry and put the baking sheet into the oven.
Electricity:	
Conventional	175–200 (preheated)
Convection	160–170 (cold)
Gas:	3–4 (preheated)
Baking time:	About 45 minutes

Scottish butter biscuits (shortbread)

(photo p. 163)

	For the pastry, sieve
375 g flour	into a mixing bowl. Add
200 g brown sugar	
1 pkt vanilla sugar	
250 g soft butter	Mix the ingredients for a moment, using the kneading attachment on the electric mixer and a low setting, then switch to high and knead thoroughly. Turn out on to the work surface and continue kneading by hand until you have a smooth ball of pastry. Shape the pastry into rolls, 2–2 ½ cm in diameter. Refrigerate until the pastry is hard. Cut the rolls into slices ½ cm thick. Arrange on a baking sheet and bake in the oven.
Electricity:	
Conventional	175–200 (preheated)
Convection	160–170 (preheated)
Gas:	3–4 (preheated)
Baking time:	About 10 minutes

Nut or coconut triangles

	For the pastry, mix
150 g flour	
½ level tsp baking powder	and sieve into a mixing bowl. Add
65 g sugar	
1 pkt vanilla sugar	
salt	
1 egg	
65 g soft margarine	Mix the ingredients for a moment, using the kneading attachment on the electric mixer and a low setting, then switch to high and knead thoroughly. Turn out on to the work surface and continue kneading by hand until you have a smooth ball of pastry. If the pastry sticks, pop it into the refrigerator for a while. Roll the pastry into a 32 × 24 cm rectangle and place on a baking sheet. Brush with
2 tbs apricot jam	
	For the filling, slowly heat
100 g butter	
100 g sugar	
1 pkt vanilla sugar	
2 tbs water	Stir in
75 g ground hazel nuts	
125 g chopped hazel nuts	
or 200 g desiccated coconut.	Leave to cool. Spread this mixture over the pastry. Pleat a piece of aluminium foil and place it across the open end of the pastry to form an edge. Put the baking sheet into the oven.
Electricity:	
Conventional	175 – 200 (preheated)
Convection	160 – 170 (cold)
Gas:	3 – 4 (preheated)
Baking time:	20 – 30 minutes Allow to cool off slightly. Cut into 8x8 cm squares, then cut these across to form triangles.
	For the glaze, melt
50 g dark glaze	
a little coconut fat	in a small bowl in a water bath over a low heat, stirring until the mixture is smooth. Brush over the pointed end of the triangles.

East German poppyseed strudel

	For the pastry, sieve
250 g flour	into a mixing bowl. Add
100 ml lukewarm water, salt	
1 small egg	
1 tbs cooking oil	Mix the ingredients for a moment, using the kneading attachment on the electric mixer and a low setting, then switch to high and knead thoroughly. Turn out on to the work surface and continue kneading by hand until you have a smooth ball of pastry. If the pastry sticks, pop it into the refrigerator for a while. Place the ball of dough on greaseproof paper inside a hot, dry pan (boil water in it beforehand), cover with a lid and leave to rest for 30 minutes.
	For the filling, pour
375 – 500 ml (3/8 – 1/2 l) boiling water	over
500 g freshly ground poppyseeds	Stir and leave to swell until you have a smooth mixture. Stir in
100 g sugar	
3 tbs honey	
1 egg	
grated peel of 1 lemon (untreated)	
100 g raisins	Peel, quarter, core and grate
250 g cooking apples	Stir into the poppyseed mixture. Roll out the strudel pastry on a large, floured cloth (table cloth). Using your hands, carefully pull the pastry until you have a transparent rectangle 50 × 70 cm. If the edges are thicker, cut them off. Spread 2/3 of the filling over the pastry, leaving about 3 cm free at the short sides. With the aid of the cloth, roll up the pastry from one of the long sides. Press the edges together firmly. Place on a greased baking sheet, brush with a little butter taken from
50 g melted butter	and bake
Electricity:	
Conventional	200 – 225 (preheated)
Convection	170 – 180 (cold)
Gas:	3 – 4 (preheated)
Baking time:	About 50 minutes Dredge the strudel with icing sugar when it has cooled off completely.

Individual fruit flans
(makes 12 – 14)

	For the pastry, mix
200 g flour 1 level tsp baking powder	and sieve into a mixing bowl. Add
75 g sugar 1 pkt vanilla sugar salt 4 drops lemon baking oil 2 tbs water 100 g soft margarine	Mix the ingredients for a moment, using the kneading attachment on the electric mixer and a low setting, then switch to high and knead thoroughly. Turn out on to the work surface and continue kneading by hand until you have a smooth ball of pastry. If the pastry sticks, pop it into the refrigerator for a while. Roll the pastry out thinly, cut out rounds 10 cm in diameter and use these to line well greased, 11 cm diameter, individual flan dishes. Prick several times with a fork and bake.
Electricity:	
Conventional	175 – 200 (preheated)
Convection	160 – 170 (preheated)
Gas:	3 – 4 (preheated)
Baking time:	12 – 15 minutes Allow to cool off. When cold, sprinkle the bases of the flans with cream stiffener to stop them from becoming soggy when filled with fruit.
	For the filling, wash, trim and drain (raspberries should only be picked over)
500 – 750 g raw fruit (e.g. strawberries, raspberries, bilberries)	Sprinkle with sugar, and leave to stand for a while
or	drain
stewed or preserved fruit (e.g. apricots, peaches, sour cherries, gooseberries, mandarin oranges)	and arrange the fruit on the flans, leaving about 1 cm free around the edge.
	For the glaze, prepare
1 pkt flan glaze sugar as instructed	

250 ml (¼ l) water or fruit juice	as directed on the packet. Pour over the fruit. Beat for ½ minute. Add
250 ml (1 pot) double cream	
1 pkt cream stiffener	
1 pkt vanilla sugar	and continue beating until stiff. Use to decorate the edges of the flans.

Fine almond biscuits

	For the pastry, mix
375 g flour	
1 level tsp baking powder	and sieve into a mixing bowl. Add
125 g sugar	
1 pkt vanilla sugar	
salt	
2 drops bitter almond baking oil	
grated peel of ½ lemon (untreated)	
1 egg	
250 g soft butter or margarine	Mix the ingredients for a moment, using the kneading attachment on the electric mixer and a low setting, then switch to high and knead thoroughly. Quickly knead in
100 g peeled, chopped almonds	on medium setting. Turn out on to the work surface and continue kneading by hand until you have a smooth ball of pastry. Roll the pastry into a rectangle 14 × 22 cm. Refrigerate overnight. Cut the pastry into strips 22 × 3.5 cm. Cut off ½ to 1 cm thick pieces. Place on a baking sheet in the oven.
Electricity:	
Conventional	175 – 200 (preheated)
Convection	160 – 170 (preheated)
Gas:	3 – 4 (preheated)
Baking time:	15 – 20 minutes
	For the glaze, melt
175 g cooking chocolate	
a little coconut fat	in a small bowl in a water bath over a low heat, stirring until the mixture is smooth. Dip the cold biscuits in the glaze so that they are half covered.

Yeast doughs and pastries

Preparation

Both fresh and dried yeast are available in the shops. If you use dried yeast, no special preparations are necessary. The yeast is added directly from the packet to the flour and carefully mixed with it (the exception to this rule is for doughs containing a large number of ingredients, such as teacake and stollen doughs, where the yeast must first be mixed with liquid). In general, baking sheets and pans should be greased. Soft margarine or butter is best for this job. Some recipes call for baking pans to be sprinkled with breadcrumbs.

The individual steps

" Sieve the flour into a mixing bowl and distribute the yeast evenly through the flour, using a fork..."
Dried yeast is preserved by means of a special process, and has the added advantage that it does not need to be dissolved in liquid or incorporated into a batter before it can be used.

"...add all the remaining ingredients to the flour..."
Yeast needs warmth to release its full raising power – milk or water should be at 37° C. The liquid should be added to the dry ingredients gradually and stirred in, to ensure that the warmth is evenly distributed through the dough.

"The following 2 steps show the preparations for making a fruity yeast cake (the same applies to stollen)." Remember, if a dough contains lots of ingredients, a starter batter must be prepared with the yeast. It is important to check that the batter with the yeast has started to rise. The batter is made by stirring together the yeast, a little sugar or honey and lukewarm milk. This mixture is left to stand for 15 minutes at room temperature. Yeast can only release its full raising power in the presence of warmth. The milk should be at body temperature, i.e. 37° C.

The other ingredients should not make contact with the yeast until the dough is being prepared. Ingredients such as salt and fat inhibit raising and should be kept near the edge of the mixing bowl and kneaded in when the flour and yeast are thoroughly combined. Yeast can break sugar down easily, but has to break down the flour (starch) first.

"...First mix the ingredients on the lowest mixer setting for a moment before switching to high and combining them thoroughly. The dough must be smooth..."
Kneading the dough ensures that the ingredients are thoroughly combined and works air into the dough. During kneading, yeast converts the **carbohydrates** sugar and flour (starch) into **carbonic acid and alcohol,** which lighten the dough. Yeast can convert sugar easily but has to break down flour (starch) first.

Yeast doughs and pastries

"...Cover the dough with cling film and leave to rise in a warm place until it has grown visibly in size (i. e. is well risen)."
Yeast doughs and pastries must not be baked as soon as they are prepared, they need to be left to rise first. Stand them in a warm place, e.g. gas or electric oven.
Gas: Preheat for 3 minutes on 8.
Switch off. Stand bowl containing dough in oven until dough is well risen.
Electricity: Switch on to 50. Stand bowl containing dough in oven until dough is well risen. Keep oven door ajar with a wooden spoon.

"...Continue as directed in the recipe (e. g. put the dough into a prepared angel cake tin, roll, shape or plait it). Always allow it to rise once more (prove) before baking."

Baking yeast doughs and pastries

Before being baked, yeast doughs and pastries should always be left in a warm place to rise or prove. This gives the dough its required lightness. Dough will rise more quickly if covered with a kitchen towel. Bake according to the directions given in the individual recipes.

Triple yeast plait
(photo 168/169)

	Sieve
500 g flour	into a mixing bowl. Add
1 pkt dried yeast	and mix carefully with the flour. Add
80 g sugar	
1 pkt vanilla sugar	
½ tsp salt	
1 pot (150 g) crème fraîche	
150 ml lukewarm milk	
75 g melted, cooled butter or margarine	Mix the ingredients for a moment, using the kneading attachment on the electric mixer and a low setting, then switch to high and knead thoroughly for 5 minutes. If the dough is sticky, add a little extra flour (not too much as the dough should be soft). Cover the dough and leave to rise in a warm place until it is well risen. Drain
4 small slices of canned pineapple	and cut them into very small pieces. Sort
100 g raisins	Slice
70 g unpeeled almonds	Remove the risen dough from the bowl and knead it thoroughly on the work surface. Divide the dough into 3 pieces. Knead the pineapple into one piece (add flour if needed), the raisins into the second piece and the almonds into the third. Roll the dough into three pieces about 35 cm long. Make into a plait and place on a greased baking sheet. Cover and leave to rise until well risen. Brush the dough with water and push the baking sheet into the oven.
Electricity:	
Conventional	175 – 200 (preheated)
Convection	160 – 170 (cold)
Gas:	3 – 4 (preheated)
Baking time:	About 35 minutes Brush the plait with water again as soon as you take it out of the oven.

Yeast doughs and pastries

Butter cake

	Sieve
375 g flour	into a mixing bowl. Add
1 pkt dried yeast	and mix carefully with the flour. Add
50 g sugar	
1 pkt vanilla sugar	
salt, 1 egg	
200 ml lukewarm milk	
50 g melted, cooled butter	Mix the ingredients for a moment, using the kneading attachment on the electric mixer and a low setting, then switch to high and knead thoroughly for 5 minutes. If the dough is sticky add a little extra flour (not too much as the dough should be soft). Cover the dough and leave to rise in a warm place until it is well risen. Remove the risen dough from the bowl and knead it thoroughly on the work surface. Roll out the dough onto a greased baking sheet. Pleat a piece of aluminium foil and place in front of the dough.
	For the topping, distribute
125 g butter	over the dough in pats, or melt and brush over. Mix
75 g sugar	
1 pkt vanilla sugar	Sprinkle on the butter with
50 g peeled chopped almonds	Leave the dough to rise again until well risen. Push the baking sheet into the oven.
Electricity:	
Conventional	200 – 225 (preheated)
Convection	170 – 180 (cold)
Gas:	4 – 5 (preheated)
Baking time:	About 15 minutes

Covered apple cake

	Sieve
500 g flour	into a mixing bowl. Add
1 pkt dried yeast	and mix carefully with the flour. Add
75 g sugar	

1 pkt vanilla sugar	
sea salt,	
75 g melted, cooled butter	
1 egg	
250 ml (¼ l) lukewarm milk	Mix the ingredients for a moment, using the kneading attachment on the electric mixer and a low setting, then switch to high and knead thoroughly for 5 minutes. Cover the dough and leave to rise in a warm place until it is well risen.
	For the filling, peel, quarter, core and cut into pieces
2 kg apples	Stew with
75 g raisins	
1 pkt vanilla sugar	
1 level tsp cinnamon	stirring frequently. Leave to cool. Remove the risen dough from the bowl and knead it thoroughly on the work surface. Roll out ⅔ of the dough on to a greased baking sheet, pushing it up a little at the edges. Spread the filling over the dough. Roll out the remaining dough to the size of the baking sheet and use it to cover the filling. Press down firmly at the sides. Prick the top several times with a fork. Leave in a warm place to rise until well risen. Push the baking sheet into the oven.
Electricity:	
Conventional	200 – 225 (preheated)
Convection	170 – 180 (cold)
Gas:	4 – 5 (preheated)
Baking time:	15 – 20 minutes
	For the glaze, sieve
125 g icing sugar	and mix to a thick paste with
2 tbs lemon juice	Brush the top of the cold apple cake with the glaze.
Tip:	Use ready made lemon fondant glaze instead of the icing glaze.

Yeast doughs and pastries

Bienenstich
(photo p. 177)

	Put
400 g finely ground wheat	
100 g finely ground spelt	into a mixing bowl. Add
1 pkt dried yeast	and mix carefully with the flour. Add
75 g honey	
sea salt, 1 egg	
250 ml (¼ l) lukewarm milk	
100 g melted, cooled butter or margarine	Mix the ingredients for a moment, using the kneading attachment on the electric mixer and a low setting, then switch to high and knead thoroughly for 5 minutes. Cover the dough and leave to rise in a warm place until it is well risen.
	For the filling, heat
100 – 125 g butter	
100 – 125 g honey	stirring continuously. Stir in
200 g peeled, chopped almonds	
2 heaped tsp finely ground wheat	Bring to the boil, remove from the heat and allow to cool stirring occasionally. Remove the risen dough from the bowl and knead it thoroughly on the work surface. Roll out on a greased baking sheet, prick several times with a fork. Pleat a piece of aluminium foil and place it in front of the dough. Spread the filling evenly over the dough (photo 1). Leave to stand in a warm place until well risen.

Continued on page 178

Yeast doughs and pastries

	Push the baking sheet into the oven.
Electricity:	
Conventional	200 (preheated)
Convection	160 – 170 (cold)
Gas:	3 – 4 (preheated)
Baking time:	15 – 20 minutes

	For the filling, prepare a pudding as instructed on the packet from
2 pkts vanilla-flavoured pudding powder 75 g sugar	
750 ml (3/4 l) milk	Leave to cool stirring occasionally. Beat
250 g (1/4 l) double cream	for 1/2 minute. Sprinkle in
1 pkt cream stiffener	Beat the cream until stiff and fold it carefully into the cold pudding. Slice the Bienenstich through horizontally (photo 2) and fill with the cream (photo 3).

Tip:	Bienenstich freezes well. Before serving, pop into a preheated oven at 200 degrees (gas 3 – 4) and reheat.

Filled, sliced ring

	Sieve
500 g flour	into a mixing bowl. Add
1 pkt dried yeast	and mix carefully with the flour. Add
100 g sugar 1 pkt vanilla sugar salt 1 egg 200 ml lukewarm milk 125 g melted, cooled butter or margarine	Mix the ingredients for a moment, using the

	kneading attachment on the electric mixer and a low setting, then switch to high and knead thoroughly for 5 minutes. If the dough is sticky, add a little extra flour (not too much as the dough should be soft).
	Cover the dough and leave to rise in a warm place until it is well risen. Remove the risen dough from the bowl, and knead it thoroughly on the work surface. Roll out to a 40 × 50 cm rectangle. Brush with
50 – 75 g soft butter or margarine	and cut through once lengthways.
	For the filling, mix together
75 g currants 125 g raisins 50 g diced candied peel 50 g peeled, chopped almonds 50 g sugar	
1 pkt vanilla sugar	Sprinkle on the dough, leaving 2 cm free near each cut edge. Roll up each piece of dough starting at the long sides. Twist them together and place on a greased baking sheet in a circle. Brush with
evaporated milk	Dip a knife in water and make cuts 1 cm deep on top of the rolls.
	Leave the ring in a warm place until well risen. Push the baking sheet into the oven.
Electricity:	
Conventional	175 – 200 (preheated)
Convection	160 – 170 (cold)
Gas:	3 – 4 (preheated)
Baking time:	25 – 35 minutes
	For the glaze, sieve
50 g icing sugar	and mix to a thick paste with
1 tbs hot water	Brush the ring with this mixture as soon as it comes out of the oven.
Variation:	Cream 200 g almond paste with 2 egg yolks and 1 tbs water and spread over the pastry after it has first been brushed with fat. Bake the ring a little longer.

Apple, crumble or plum cake
(photo p. 181)

	Sieve
500 g flour	into a mixing bowl. Add
1 pkt dried yeast	and mix carefully with the flour. Add
75 g sugar	
1 pkt vanilla sugar	
salt	
250 ml (¼ l)lukewarm milk	
75 – 100 g melted, cooled butter or margarine	Mix the ingredients for a moment, using the kneading attachment on the electric mixer and a low setting, then switch to high and knead thoroughly for 5 minutes. If the dough is sticky, add a little extra flour (not too much as the dough should be soft). Cover the dough and leave to rise in a warm place until it is well risen. Remove the risen dough from the bowl and knead it thoroughly on the work surface. Roll out on a greased baking sheet. Pleat a piece of aluminium foil and place it in front of the dough.
	For the crumble cake filling, sieve
300 g flour	into a bowl and mix with
150 g sugar	
1 pkt vanilla sugar	
150 – 200 g soft butter.	Knead with the mixer until the crumbs are the desired size. Sprinkle evenly on the dough. Leave the dough in a warm place until it is well risen. Push the baking sheet into the oven.
Electricity:	
Conventional	200 – 225 (preheated)
Convection	170 – 180 (cold)
Gas:	4 – 5 (preheated)
Baking time:	15 – 20 minutes
	For the apple cake, peel, quarter, core and thickly slice
1 ½ kg apples	Distribute these evenly over the dough and sprinkle with
20 g peeled, split almonds	

Continued on page 182

	Leave the dough in a warm place until it is well risen. Push the baking sheet into the oven.
Electricity:	
Conventional	200 – 225 (preheated)
Convection	170 (cold)
Gas:	4 – 5 (preheated)
Baking time:	20 – 30 minutes
	For the apricot glaze, bring
a good 3 tbs of apricot jam	
1 tbs water	to the boil, stirring continuously. Brush over the apple cake as soon as it comes out of the oven.
	For the plum cake, wash, drain, dry and stone
3 kg plums	Arrange like scales on the dough, with the cut surfaces facing upwards. Leave the dough in a warm place until it is well risen. Push the baking sheet into the oven.
Electricity:	
Conventional	200 – 225 (preheated)
Convection	170 (cold)
Gas:	4 – 5 (preheated)
Baking time:	20 – 30 minutes
	Allow the cake to cool off a little before sprinkling with
sugar	

Apricot cake with semolina topping
(wholefood cake)

	For the dough, put
300 g finely ground wheat	
100 g finely ground buckwheat	into a mixing bowl. Add
1 pkt dried yeast	and mix carefully with the flour. Add
75 g honey	
sea salt	
200 ml lukewarm milk	

75 g melted, cooled butter or margarine	Mix the ingredients for a moment, using the kneading attachment on the electric mixer and a low setting, then switch to high and knead thoroughly for 5 minutes. Cover the dough and leave to rise in a warm place until it is well risen.
	For the semolina topping, bring
750 ml (¾ l) milk 75 g butter 150 g honey sea salt 3 – 4 pieces of lemon peel (untreated)	to the boil. Sprinkle in
75 g wholemeal semolina	stirring continuously. Bring to the boil again, simmer for about 5 minutes then remove from heat. Beat together
4 egg yolks 3 tbs milk	and stir into the semolina. Wash, stone and cut in half
1 ½ kg ripe apricots	Remove the risen dough from the bowl and knead it thoroughly on the work surface. Roll out on a greased baking sheet and sprinkle with
3 tbs wholemeal breadcrumbs	Arrange the apricot halves on top. Leave the dough in a warm place until well risen. Beat
4 egg-whites	until stiff and carefully fold into the semolina. Spread the semolina evenly over the apricots. Push the baking sheet into the oven.
Electricity:	
Conventional	175 – 200 (preheated)
Convection	160 (preheated)
Gas:	3 – 4 (preheated)
Baking time:	40 – 45 minutes

Tip: Wholemeal cake should be removed from the baking sheet while still warm, cut into quarters and left to cool on a wire rack.

Yeast doughs and pastries

Buchteln

(photo p. 185)

	Sieve
500 g flour	into a mixing bowl. Add
1 pkt dried yeast	and mix carefully with the flour. Add
125 g sugar	
1 pkt vanilla sugar	
4 drops lemon-flavoured baking oil	
salt	
1 egg	
200 ml lukewarm milk	
100 g melted, cooled butter or margarine	Mix the ingredients for a moment, using the kneading attachment on the electric mixer and a low setting, then switch to high and knead thoroughly for 5 minutes. Cover the dough and leave to rise in a warm place until it is well risen. Remove the risen dough from the bowl and knead it thoroughly on the work surface. Shape dough into a roll, cut into 12 equal sized pieces and roll these into balls. Melt
50–75 g butter	in a rectangular baking pan (about 20 × 30 cm). Turn the balls in the butter until covered all over. Put them into the baking pan (not too close together) and leave to rise in a warm place until well risen. Push into the oven on the wire shelf.
Electricity:	
Conventional	200–225 (preheated)
Convection	170–180 (cold)
Gas:	3–4 (cold)
Baking time:	20–30 minutes If liked, the finished Buchteln can be dredged with
icing sugar	
Accompaniment:	stewed fruit or vanilla sauce
Tip:	Buchteln are delicious at teatime, but can also be served as a light lunch in summer. Confectioner's snow can be used instead of icing sugar.

Yeast doughs and pastries

Yeast doughs and pastries

Yeast stollen
(wholefood loaf)

	Cover
350 g sultanas	
150 g currants	with
6 tbs rum	Leave to stand for several hours or overnight.
	For the dough, put
375 g finely ground wheat	
125 g finely ground spelt	
100 g honey	
sea salt	
2 pinches ground cardamom	
2 pinches ground cloves	
2 pinches ground mace	into a mixing bowl. Add
250 g soft butter	cut into pieces. Dissolve
1 cube (42 g) fresh yeast	in
200 ml (1/5 l) lukewarm milk	and add to the other ingredients. Mix the ingredients for a moment, using the kneading attachment on the electric mixer and a low setting, then switch to high and knead thoroughly for 5 minutes. Cover the dough and leave to rise in a warm place until it is well risen. Remove the risen dough from the bowl and knead in the rum fruit and
100 g diced candied lemon peel	
150 g chopped almonds	Shape the dough into a loaf, place on a baking sheet lined with greaseproof paper and leave in a warm place until well risen. Push the baking sheet into the oven.
Electricity:	
Conventional	Preheat to 250, bake at 150 – 175
Convection	Preheat to 200, bake at 140 – 150
Baking time:	About 70 minutes Switch off oven and leave for 5 minutes
Gas:	2 – 3 (preheated)
Baking time:	60 – 70 minutes
	Melt
100 g butter	
1 tbs honey	Brush over the stollen as soon as it comes out of the oven.

Yeast Ring Mould

	Dissolve
1 pkt dried yeast	
1 tsp sugar	in
200 ml lukewarm double cream	in a small bowl. Leave to stand for about 15 minutes at room temperature. Sieve
500 g flour	into a mixing bowl. Make a well in the centre. Around the edges of the flour put
125 g sugar	
1 pkt vanilla sugar	
6 drops lemon-flavoured baking oil	
salt	
75 g peeled, ground almonds	
3 eggs	
200 g melted, cooled butter or margarine	Pour the yeast mixture into the well. Mix the ingredients for a moment, using the kneading attachment on the electric mixer and a low setting, then switch to high and knead thoroughly for 5 minutes. Cover the dough and leave to rise in a warm place until it is well risen. Knead again thoroughly. Quickly knead in
150 g raisins	on medium setting. Transfer the dough to a 24 cm diameter greased ring or angel cake mould, sprinkled with
breadcrumbs	Leave to stand in a warm place until well risen. Push the mould into the oven on the wire shelf.
Electricity:	
Conventional	175 – 200 (preheated)
Convection	160 – 170 (cold)
Gas:	2 – 3 (cold)
Baking time:	About 50 minutes

Danish pastry

Preparations

Generally speaking no special preparations are needed when baking with dried yeast. The yeast is added from the packet directly to the flour and carefully distributed with a spoon. Baking sheets should be greased with soft butter or margarine.

The individual steps

"...sieve the flour into a mixing bowl and stir the yeast in evenly..."
The yeast is preserved by means of a special process and saves time because it does not need to be dissolved or incorporated into a starter batter before use.

"...add all the remaining ingredients to the flour..."
The yeast dough that is the basis for Danish pastry is prepared "cold". This means that the fat and milk need not be lukewarm. Like puff pastry, Danish pastry calls for the use of cold ingredients.

"...Using the kneading attachment on the mixer, mix the ingredients briefly on a low setting, switch to high and knead for 5 minutes. The dough must be smooth..."

Kneading the yeast dough ensures that all the ingredients are well combined and works air into the dough. During kneading, the yeast converts the carbohydrates sugar and flour (starch) into carbolic acid and alcohol, which lighten the dough. Yeast can convert sugar quickly, but needs more time for flour (starch), which has to be broken down first. Leave the dough to rest for 5 minutes at room temperature.

"...Roll out the dough, arrange butter over half, fold together..."

Roll out the dough to a 25 × 40 cm rectangle on a floured work surface. Arrange **thin slices of cold butter** over half (25 × 20 cm) the dough, fold the other half of the pastry over the butter and press down lightly with the rolling pin.

"...Roll out again, fold up, refrigerate."

Place the pastry parcel on the work surface, with the long edge lined up with the edge of the table. Roll out to a 25 × 40 cm rectangle again. Fold the short ends to the middle so that they meet. Fold over again from the long side so that you have 4 layers of pastry. Leave in the refrigerator for 15 minutes.

Danish pastry

"Roll pastry out again, fold, refrigerate."
Line up the long edge of the pastry package with the edge of the table and roll out to a 25 × 40 cm rectangle. Fold the short ends to the middle so that they meet.
Fold over again from the long side so that you have 4 layers of pastry once more. Leave in the refrigerator for a further 15 minutes.

This dough can be used to make a large variety of pastries. Follow the instructions in the recipe with regard to rolling out and shaping, and leave to rest for 15 minutes at room temperature.

Baking Danish pastries

Danish pastry is a mixture of yeast dough and puff pastry. It is very important to cool the pastry for 15 minutes after each step has been completed. When finally shaped, all Danish pastry should be covered and allowed to rest for a further 15 minutes at room temperature. This allows the fat to combine better with the other ingredients. Bake the pastries as directed in the recipes.

Brunswick butter pretzels

(makes about 20, photo p. 188/189)

	For the pastry, sieve
375 g flour	into a mixing bowl, mix carefully with
1 pkt dried yeast	Add
100 g sugar	
1 pkt vanilla sugar	
salt	
1 egg	
125 ml (1/8 l) lukewarm milk	
50 g melted, cooled butter or margarine	Using the kneading attachment on the mixer, mix the ingredients briefly on a low setting, switch to high and knead for 5 minutes, finally kneading in
250 g butter	in small pieces. Put the dough into the refrigerator until well cooled.
	Cover
1 pkt (300 g) frozen puff pastry	and allow to thaw at room temperature. Roll the yeast dough out to a 40 × 30 cm rectangle, lay 3 slices of puff pastry on one half of the dough, and cover with the other half. Roll out so that the remaining 2 slices of puff pastry cover half the dough, fold over, press down, and refrigerate for at least 1 hour. Roll out the pastry to a 55 × 30 cm rectangle, cut into strips 1 ½ cm wide, twist the strips into spirals and shape into pretzels. Place on a greased baking sheet, and leave to rest for 15 minutes at room temperature until the pretzels have visibly increased in size. Mix
1 egg yolk	
1 ½–2 tbs evaporated milk	Brush the pretzels with this mixture and sprinkle with
25 g peeled, chopped almonds	
25 g coarse granulated sugar	Push the baking sheet into the oven.
Electricity:	
Conventional	200–225 (preheated)
Convection	180 (preheated)
Gas:	4–5 (preheated)
Baking time:	Approx. 15 minutes
	Before serving, sprinkle the pretzels with
icing sugar	

Rosettes

(makes 25, photo p. 195)

For the pastry, sieve
375 g flour into a mixing bowl, and mix carefully with
1 pkt dried yeast. Add
50 g sugar
1 pkt vanilla sugar
salt
1 egg
50 g butter cut into pieces
200 ml cold milk. Using the kneading attachment on the mixer, mix the ingredients briefly on a low setting, switch to high and knead for 5 minutes (photo 1). Leave to rest for 5 minutes at room temperature. Roll out the dough to a 25 × 40 cm rectangle. Slice
150 g cold butter. Arrange the butter over half the dough (25 × 20 cm), fold over the other half to cover the butter, and press down lightly with a rolling pin. Line up the long edge of the pastry parcel with the edge of the table, and roll out until 25 × 40 cm again. Fold the short edges to the middle so that they touch.

Fold the pastry in half from the long edge again so that you have 4 layers of pastry. Put the pastry in the refrigerator for 15 minutes. Line up the long edge of the pastry parcel with the edge of the table again, and roll and fold as described above, finishing with 4 layers of pastry. Refrigerate for a further 15 minutes.

For the filling, bring to the boil
125 ml (1/8 l) milk
100 g sugar

Continued on page 196

Danish pastry

1 pkt vanilla sugar	
salt	Stir in
250 g ground hazel nuts	
25 g breadcrumbs	
½ tsp ground cinnamon	
2 tbs rum	Allow to cool. Stir in
1 egg	Roll the pastry to a 40 × 50 cm rectangle, spread with the filling, roll up and cut into slices about 2 cm thick (photo 2). Arrange the slices on a greased baking sheet and leave to stand at room temperature for 15–30 minutes until visibly increased in size. Using scissors, make 5 cuts in each slice (photo 3). Push the baking sheet into the oven.
Electricity:	
Conventional	200–225 (preheated)
Convection	170–180 (cold)
Gas:	4 (preheated)
Baking time:	Approx. 20 minutes
	As soon as the rosettes come out of the oven, brush them with
50 g melted butter	and sprinkle with
sugar	

Danish ring

	For the pastry, sieve
375 g flour	into a mixing bowl. Mix carefully with
1 pkt dried yeast	Add
50 g sugar	
1 pkt vanilla sugar	
salt	
1 egg	
50 g butter cut into pieces	
200 ml cold milk	Using the kneading attachment on the mixer, mix the ingredients briefly on a low setting, switch to high and knead for 5 minutes. Leave to rest for 5 minutes at room temperature. Roll out the dough to a 25 × 40 cm rectangle. Slice

Danish pastry

150 g cold butter	Arrange the butter over half the dough (25 × 20 cm), fold over the other half to cover the butter, press down lightly with a rolling pin. Line up the long edge of the pastry parcel with the edge of the table and roll out until 25 × 40 cm again. Fold the short edges to the middle so that they touch. Fold the pastry in half from the long edge again so that you have 4 layers of pastry. Put the pastry in the refrigerator for 15 minutes. Line up the long edge of the pastry parcel with the edge of the table again, and roll and fold as described above, finishing with 4 layers of pastry. Refrigerate for a further 15 minutes.
	For the filling, cream
200 g almond paste	
50 g soft butter	using the electric mixer with the whisk attachment. Stir in
1 tbs rum	Roll out the dough to a 50 × 40 cm rectangle, spread with the marzipan mixture. Sprinkle with
175 g raisins	
50 g peeled, chopped almonds	Cut the dough through once lengthways. Roll up each piece form the long side, twist the rolls together and form into a ring on a greased baking sheet. Leave to stand for 15 minutes at room temperature. Push the baking sheet into the oven.
Electricity:	
Conventional	175 – 200 (preheated)
Convection	160 – 170 (cold)
Gas:	3 – 4 (preheated)
Baking time:	35 – 40 minutes
	For the apricot glaze push
1 tbs apricot jam	through a sieve. Bring to the boil with
1 tbs water	Brush the ring with this mixture as soon as it comes out of the oven. Leave to cool a little.
	For the glaze, sieve
50 g icing sugar	Mix with
1 – 2 tbs rum	until you have a smooth, thin paste. Brush over the ring and sprinkle with
peeled, chopped almonds	

Danish pastry

Colourful Danish pastries

(photo p. 199)

	Prepare the pastry as described for the
Danish ring on p. 196	
	For the filling, prepare a pudding from
1 pkt vanilla-flavoured pudding powder 25 g sugar 250 ml (¼) milk	Leave to cool, stirring occasionally. Roll out the dough to a 48 × 18 cm rectangle, cut into 8 × 9 cm squares, place on a baking sheet and put 2 tsp cold pudding into the centre of each square. Decorate with
peach slices cherries	Make cuts in the corners of the squares, and leave to rest for 15 minutes at room temperature. Push the baking sheet into the oven.
Electricity:	
Conventional	200 – 225 (preheated)
Convection	180 (preheated)
Gas:	4 (preheated)
Baking time:	About 15 minutes
	For the glaze, sieve
100 g icing sugar	Mix with
4 tbs peach juice	until you have a smooth, thin paste. Brush over the pastries as soon as they come out of the oven, not forgetting the centre.
Tip:	The icing glace can be replaced with a ready made, lemon-flavoured fondant glaze (tube).

Quark and oil pastry

Preparation

Mix and sieve flour and baking powder.
Mixing and sieving aerate the flour and distribute the baking powder evenly. This makes the pastry lighter.

Baking sheets and pans must be greased for use with quark and oil pastry.
Use soft butter or margarine for this, distributing it carefully with a brush.

The individual steps

"Mix the sieved flour and baking powder, quark, milk, egg, oil, sugar, honey, vanilla sugar and salt, as specified in the recipe, for about 1 minute with the electric mixer on its highest setting."
Put the ingredients into the mixing bowl in the sequence indicated in the recipe (always break eggs into a cup first to check that they are fresh). Oil is an essential ingredient of this pastry and must not be replaced by solid fat. Any neutral tasting cooking oil may be used.

With floured hands, shape the dough into a roll on the work surface. If the dough is too soft, a little flour may be added (not too much otherwise the pastry will be hard).

Quark and oil pastry

This dough can be used for a variety of pastries. It can be rolled out, shaped, filled or topped. For small pastries, roll the dough out a good ½ cm thick, cut into squares, and put a little jam in the centre of each square. Fold the squares into triangles, envelopes, etc., brush with milk, and bake on a greased baking sheet.

Baking quark and oil pastries

Bake all quark and oil pastries as instructed in the recipes. As soon as the pastry comes out of the oven it must be removed from the baking sheet or pan and transferred to a cake rack to cool. Quark and oil pastry should be eaten as fresh as possible.

Orange and marzipan plaits

(photo p. 200/201)

	For the filling, cream together
200 g almond paste 50 g soft butter 2 tbs orange marmalade grated peel of ½ orange (untreated) or 1 tsp powdered orange peel	
	For the pastry, sieve
300 g flour	
1 pkt baking powder	into a mixing bowl. Add
150 g quark	

Quark and oil pastry

6 tbs milk
6 tbs cooking oil
75 g sugar
1 pkt vanilla sugar
salt — Using an electric mixer with kneading attachment on its highest setting, mix the ingredients for about 1 minute. Turn out on to the work surface and shape into a roll.
Roll out to a 36 × 48 cm rectangle and cut into 12 × 12 cm squares.
Place some of the filling on to one half of each square leaving a free strip of ½ to 1 cm all round. Brush the edges with

beaten egg-white — Fold the uncovered pastry over the filling and press edges together firmly.
Cut each pastry twice lengthways, stopping 1 cm before the end. Plait the resulting three strips, pressing the ends together firmly.
Place the plaits on a baking sheet lined with greaseproof paper.
Beat together

1 egg yolk
1 tbs milk — Brush the pastry with this mixture. Push the baking sheet into the oven.

Electricity:
Conventional 175 – 200 (preheated)
Convection 160 – 170 (cold)
Gas: 3 – 4 (preheated)
Baking time: 15 – 20 minutes

For the glaze, sieve
100 g icing sugar — Mix with
2 – 3 tbs orange juice — Brush over the pastries as soon as they come out of the oven.

Quark and apple cake with crumble topping
(wholefood cake)

For the pastry, finely grind
300 g wheat — Put into a mixing bowl with
1 pkt baking powder — Mix well. Add

Quark and oil pastry

150 g quark 5 tbs milk 6 tbs cooking oil 75 g honey sea salt	Using an electric mixer with kneading attachment on its highest setting, mix the ingredients for about 1 minute. Turn out on to the work surface and shape into a roll. Roll out on a greased baking sheet. Pleat a strip of aluminium foil and lay in front of the pastry.
	For the filling, peel, quarter, core and slice
1 ½ kg cooking apples	and arrange them like scales on the pastry. With an electric mixer cream
150 g soft butter	Gradually add
200 g honey juice and grated yellow peel of 1 lemon (untreated) 4 egg yolks 850 g low fat quark	
3 tbs wholewheat semolina	Beat
5 egg-whites	until stiff, and carefully fold into the quark mixture. Spread over the apples.
	For the crumble, finely grind
250 g wheat	Using the kneading attachment on the electric mixer, mix with
100 g ground hazel nuts 2 tbs sesame seeds 150 g honey ground cinnamon 1 egg yolk	
150 – 200 g soft butter	until you have crumbs. Distribute these evenly over the quark mixture. Push the baking sheet into the oven.
Electricity:	
Conventional	175 (preheated)
Convection	150 (cold)
Gas:	3 (preheated)
Baking time:	About 1 hour

Quark and oil pastry

Redcurrant cheesecake with meringue
(photo p. 207)

	For the pastry, sieve
300 g wheat	
1 pkt baking powder	into a mixing bowl. Add
150 g quark	
6 tbs milk	
6 tbs cooking oil	
75 g sugar	
1 pkt vanilla sugar	
salt	Using an electric mixer with kneading attachment on its highest setting (photo 1), mix the ingredients for about 1 minute. Turn out on to the work surface and shape into a roll. Roll out ½ cm thick on to a greased baking sheet. Pleat a strip of aluminium foil and lay in front of the pastry.
	For the filling, wash, drain and strip
750 g redcurrants	Mix
750 g quark	
200 g sugar	
1 pkt vanilla sugar	
3 eggs	
2 egg yolks	
50 g melted butter	
50 g cornflour	Fold the redcurrants into the quark mixture and spread over the pastry (photo 2). Smooth the surface, and push the baking sheet into the oven.

Continued on page 208

Quark and oil pastry

Electricity:	
Conventional	175 – 200 (preheated)
Convection	160 – 170 (preheated)
Gas:	3 – 4 (preheated)
Baking time:	About 25 minutes
	For the meringue beat
2 egg-whites	until so stiff that a cut made in the surface with a knife remains visible. Gradually beat in
100 g sugar	Spread the egg-white mixture over the quark (photo 3). Sprinkle with
20 g peeled, chopped almonds	Push into the oven.
Electricity:	
Conventional	200 – 225 (preheated)
Convection	200 – 225 (cold)
Gas:	4 – 5 (preheated)
Baking time:	About 5 minutes

Kolatsch tarts

(makes 20 wholefood cakes) (photo p. 209)

	For the pastry, finely grind
400 g wheat	Put into a mixing bowl with
1 pkt plus 1 level tsp baking powder	Mix well. Add
200 g quark	
6 tbs milk	
100 ml cooking oil	
75 g honey	
sea salt	
1 egg	Using an electric mixer with kneading attachment on its highest setting, mix the ingredients for about 1 minute. Turn out on to the work surface and shape into a roll.
	For filling I, mix together
300 g low fat quark	
50 g soft butter	
75 g honey	
20 g arrowroot	

Continued on page 210

Quark and oil pastry

	with
1 egg	
	For filling II, bring to the boil
200 ml milk	
75 g honey	Stir in
200 g freshly ground poppyseeds	
1 tbs Graham breadcrumbs	Leave to cool.
	For filling III, stir
2 tbs thick plum preserve	until smooth. Cut the pastry into 12 pieces, roll these into balls, and then flatten them from the centre out, leaving a low standing edge. Place the pastry on a greased baking sheet. Put 1 tsp plum preserve into the centre of each. Surround this with 1 tsp poppyseed followed by 1 tsp quark. Push the baking sheet into the oven.
Electricity:	
Conventional	200 (preheated)
Convection	160 – 170 (preheated)
Baking time:	18 – 20 minutes
Gas:	3 – 4 (preheated)
Baking time:	5 – 10 minutes
	For the apricot glaze, push
3 heaped tbs apricot jam	sweetened with honey through a sieve, and mix with
4 tbs water	Boil in a small pan until well reduced. Spread over the cold tarts. Sprinkle with
40 g peeled, chopped, toasted almonds	

Egg cake

	For the pastry, sieve
250 g wheat	
3 level tsp baking powder	into a mixing bowl. Add
125 g quark	
4 tbs milk	
4 tbs cooking oil	

Quark and oil pastry

60 g sugar	
1 pkt vanilla sugar	
salt	Using an electric mixer with kneading attachment on its highest setting, mix the ingredients for about 1 minute. Turn out on to the work surface and shape into a roll. Roll out on a greased baking sheet. Pleat a strip of aluminium foil and lay in front of the pastry.
	For the quark filling mix together well
500 g quark	
30 g soft butter	
80 g sugar	
1 egg	
2 drops bitter almond-flavoured baking oil	
2 tbs milk	
1 pkt cheesecake stiffener	
40 g raisins	Spread the mixture evenly over the pastry.
	For the egg cream, prepare a pudding as instructed on the packet (but using only 250 ml milk), from
1 pkt vanilla sauce	
30 g sugar	
250 ml (1/4 l) milk	Leave to cool, stirring frequently. Cream
100 g butter	Gradually stir in
75 g sieved icing sugar	
3 egg yolks	Beat
3 egg-whites	until stiff, and fold carefully into the cream. Spread the cream over the quark mixture and push the baking sheet into the oven.
Electricity:	
Conventional	175 – 200 (preheated)
Convection	160 – 170 (cold)
Gas:	3 – 4 (preheated)
Baking time:	About 30 minutes

Puff Pastry

Making puff pastry at home takes a lot of time and trouble, and good results are not always guaranteed. The pastry has to puff up into layers, and this depends very largely on using the right sort of fat, which is normally only available from bakers. For this reason it is advisable to buy frozen puff pastry, which is very good and guarantees the results you want.

Strawberry slices

(photo p. 212/213)

	For the pastry, allow
1 pkt (300 g) frozen puff pastry	to thaw at room temperature
	For the filling, prepare a pudding with
1 pkt vanilla-flavoured pudding powder	
40 g sugar	
125 ml (1/8 l) milk	
250 g (1 pot) double cream	following the instructions on the packet. Leave to cool, stirring occasionally.
	For the filling, wash, drain, trim and cut in half
750 g strawberries	Sprinkle with
50 g sugar	Leave to draw juice. Lay the puff pastry sheets on top of each other and roll out to a 34x30 cm rectangle. Cut out 2 30x14 cm rectangles, and place on a baking sheet that has been rinsed with water. Cut the remaining pastry into narrow strips, twist these together and place them around the edges of the pastry, after first brushing it with
evaporated milk	Brush with evaporated milk. Prick the pastry several times with a fork, pricking it again if necessary during baking. Push the baking sheet into the oven.
Electricity:	
Conventional	200 – 225 (preheated)
Convection	180 (preheated)
Gas:	4 – 5 (preheated)

Baking time: 15 – 20 minutes
Remove the pastry from the baking sheet as soon as it comes out of the oven, and leave on a wire rack to cool. Spread with the pudding. Drain the strawberries well and arrange on the pudding like scales.

For the glaze, prepare

1 pkt fruit flan glaze
30 g sugar
250 ml (¼ l) strawberry juice (made up with water)

as instructed on the packet. Pour over the strawberries, sprinkle the long edges with

15 g peeled, chopped almonds

Cherry slices

For the pastry, allow

2 pkt (600 g = 10 sheets) frozen puff pastry

to thaw at room temperature. Place 5 pastry slices on a baking sheet that has been rinsed with water. Push the baking sheet into the oven.

Electricity:
Conventional 225 (preheated)
Convection 170 – 180 (preheated)
Gas: 4 (preheated)
Baking time: About 15 minutes
Bake the remaining 5 slices in the same way. Allow to cool. Carefully split each pastry slice horizontally with a breadknife.

For the filling, wash, drain, trim and stone

1 ½ kg sour cherries

Bring to the boil with

125 ml (⅛ l) water
200 g sugar
2 pkt vanilla sugar
2 sticks of cinnamon
peel of 1 lemon (untreated)

and stew for about 8 minutes,

or drain

about 900 g preserved sour cherries

reserving the juice, and measure off 500 ml (½ l).

	Put 2 tsp of juice aside, and heat the remainder. Mix
50 g cornflour	
4 tbs Kirsch	and stir into the cherry juice. Boil up briefly, stir in the cherries, and leave to cool. Distribute the cherries over half the pastry slices. Beat
500 g (2 pots) double cream	for ½ minute. Mix together
2 pkt cream stiffener	
60 g sieved icing sugar	
1 pkt vanilla sugar	Sprinkle into the cream and beat until stiff. Beat in
4 tbs Kirsch	Spoon the cream into a piping bag with a star shaped nozzle, and pipe thickly over the cherries.
	For the glaze, mix
75 g sieved icing sugar	
2 tsp cherry juice	
1 tsp Kirsch	to a smooth paste, and brush on to the unfilled pastry slices. Leave to a dry a little, then place on the cream as lids.

Filled shoe soles

(photo p. 217)

	For the pastry, allow
1 pkt (300 g) frozen puff pastry	to thaw at room temperature. Lay the thawed slices on top of each other, and roll out thinly. Cut out rounds with a pastry cutter 6 cm in diameter. Place the rounds on
sugar	and roll out to ovals. Place the ovals on a baking sheet that has been rinsed with water. Push the baking sheet into the oven.
Electricity:	
Conventional	200 – 225 (preheated)
Convection	170 – 180 (preheated)
Gas:	4 – 5 (preheated)
Baking time:	About 10 minutes
	For the filling, beat
250 g (1 pot) double cream	for ½ minute. Mix together
1 pkt vanilla sugar	
1 pkt cream stiffener	Sprinkle into the cream, and beat until stiff. Add
Kirsch	to taste. Pipe cream on to half of the "shoe soles". Cover with the other soles.

Puff Pastry

Almond bows

(photo p. 219)

	For the pastry, allow
1 pkt (300 g) frozen puff pastry	to thaw at room temperature. Lay the thawed slices on top of each other, and roll out to a rectangle 50x35 cm.
	For the filling, cream
200 g almond paste	
1 tbs apricot jam	
50 g soft butter	using an electric mixer. Spread the mixture on half the pastry (photo 1). Place the other half on top to make a rectangle 25x35 cm. Cut into strips 1 ½ cm wide and 25 cm long (photo 2). Tie the strips into loose knots and place on a baking sheet that has been rinsed with water (photo 3). Brush with
evaporated milk	Sprinkle with
about 20 g peeled, chopped almonds	Push the baking sheet into the oven.
Electricity:	
Conventional	200 – 225 (preheated)
Convection	170 – 180 (preheated)
Gas:	4 – 5 (preheated)
Baking time:	About 15 minutes
	Dust the almond bows with
confectioner's snow	before serving.

Choux Pastry

Preparation

Choux pastry is baked on a lightly greased, floured baking sheet.
Sieve a little flour on to one half of the baking sheet. Knock the uncovered half of the baking sheet against the table to distribute the flour evenly and discard any excess.

Sieve flour and cornflour.
Mixing and sieving flour and cornflour (do not sieve wholemeal flour) ensures that these ingredients are well combined and incorporates air. In view of the following step, it is advisable to sieve these two ingredients on to a piece of greaseproof paper. If you use wholemeal flour, weigh it and place ready for use.

The individual steps

"Bring water and fat to the boil in a long handled saucepan. Remove the pan from the heat and add the sieved flour and cornflour mixture all at once..."
It is important to make sure that the flour and cornflour mixture do not form lumps during cooking. This is why the pan must be removed from the heat and the entire quantity of flour and cornflour must added at once.

"...and stir until the ingredients form a ball..."
As soon as the flour and cornflour are in the hot liquid, stir vigorously until they form a smooth ball.

"...heat this for a further minute, stirring continuously..."
This extra heating makes the dough firmer. A thin skin will form on the bottom of the pan. This is a sign that the dough has been heated for long enough.

"...put the hot dough into a mixing bowl..."
The dough must be kneaded with the electric mixer, and this is easier if it is first transferred to a mixing bowl.

Choux Pastry

"...gradually work in the eggs, using the highest setting on the mixer..."
The eggs are worked into the hot dough. Break each one into a cup first to check whether it is fresh. Work the eggs in gradually, beating well between additions. They must be thoroughly incorporated in the mixture.

"...enough egg has been added when the mixture is glossy and drops heavily from a spoon..."
Because eggs vary in size, it is as well to check the consistency of the dough before adding the last egg. If it is very glossy and drops heavily from a spoon, no further egg need be added. If the mixture is too soft, the pastries will spread. Just add as much of the last egg as necessary.

"...Knead the baking powder into the cold dough."
Baking powder should not come into contact with heat before baking, as this would set off its raising power prematurely. This is why, in choux pastry, baking powder is not mixed with the flour.

If choux pastry is to be used for cream puffs, use 2 teaspoons to make small heaps of dough on a prepared baking sheet, or pipe the dough on with a piping bag. If the pastry is to be deep fried, pieces can be removed with 2 teaspoons, or rings can be piped on to greased paper and put into the hot fat.

Baking choux pastries

All choux pastries must be baked according to the instructions in the relevant recipes. The oven may not be opened until baking time has almost ended, as the pastries could otherwise collapse. If the pastry is to be deep fried, the fat must be hot enough to prevent the pastries from soaking it up. You can check fat for the correct temperature by holding a wooden spoon in it. Small bubbles must form around the spoon handle (s. Deep fried pastries, p. 234).

Choux Pastry

Choux gateau

(photo p. 221/222)

	For the kneaded pastry, sieve
150 g flour	
40 g sugar	
1 pkt vanilla sugar	into a mixing bowl and add
100 g soft butter	Using the kneading attachment on the mixer, knead the ingredients on a low setting, switching to high. Remove from the mixing bowl and knead on the work surface until you have a smooth ball. If the pastry sticks, refrigerate it for a while. Roll the pastry out thinly and use it to line a springform pan (28 cm diameter, base greased). Prick several times with a fork, and bake in the springform pan on the wire shelf in the oven.
Electricity:	
Conventional	200 – 225 (preheated)
Convection	170 – 180 (preheated)
Gas:	3 – 4 (preheated)
Baking time:	About 15 minutes
	When baking is finished, loosen the pastry from the base of the springform pan, allow to cool, then transfer to a cake stand.
	For the choux pastry, bring to the boil
125 ml (⅛ l) water	
25 g margarine	in a long handled saucepan. Mix together
75 g flour	
15 g cornflour	Remove saucepan from heat, and add flour all at once. Stir until pastry comes away from the sides of the pan in a smooth ball. Return to the heat for a further minutes, stirring continuously. Transfer the hot pastry to a mixing bowl. Using the kneading attachment on the electric mixer, and the highest setting, gradually work in
2 – 3 eggs	Enough egg has been added when the pastry is very glossy and has a heavy dropping consistency. Work
1 pinch baking powder	into the cold pastry. Bake 3 layers with the pastry. To do this spread a third of the pastry on each of 3 greased and floured springform baking pan bases (28 cm diameter), making sure the pastry is not too thin at the edges, otherwise it will be too dark when baked. Bake each flan until golden, without the springform ring.

Electricity:	
Conventional	200 – 225 (preheated)
Convection	170 – 180 (cold)
Gas:	3 – 4 (preheated)
Baking time:	20 – 25 minutes Remove the layers from the baking pans as soon as they come out of the oven, and place separately on a wire rack to cool. (This is important, as it permits the steam to escape).
	For the filling, drain
250 g stoned, stewed sour cherries	Measure off 250 ml (¼ l) juice (make up with water if necessary). Mix 4 tbs of the juice with
30 g cornflour	Bring the remaining juice to the boil. Remove pan from heat and stir in the cornflour mixture. Bring to the boil again briefly. Stir in the cherries. Leave to cool. If necessary, sweeten with
sugar	Beat
500 g (2 pots) double cream	for ½ minute. Sieve
25 g icing sugar	Mix with
1 pkt vanilla sugar	
2 pkt cream stiffener	and continue beating cream until stiff. Spread the pastry base with a thin layer of
redcurrant jelly	Cover with a choux layer. Cover this with half the cherries and ⅓ of the whipped cream. Put the second choux layer on top and cover with the remaining cherries and cream. Break up the third layer and distribute over the cream. Dust with
icing sugar	

Eclairs

(photo p. 229)

	For the choux pastry, bring to the boil
125 ml (⅛ l) water	
25 g margarine or butter	in a long handled saucepan. Mix together
75 g flour	
15 g cornflour	Remove saucepan from heat and add flour all at once. Stir until pastry comes away from the sides of the pan in a smooth ball. Return to the heat for a further minute, stirring continuously. Transfer the hot pastry to a mixing bowl. Using the kneading attachment on the electric mixer, and the highest setting, gradually work in

Continued on page 228

Choux Pastry

2-3 eggs	Enough egg has been added when the pastry is very glossy and has a heavy dropping consistency. Work
1 pinch baking powder	into the cold pastry. Transfer the mixture into a piping bag (large serrated nozzle) and pipe strips, 6 cm long, on to a greased and floured baking sheet (photo 1), or pipe two finger-long strips next to each other and a third on top. Push into the oven.
Electricity:	
Conventional	200 – 225 (preheated)
Convection	170 – 180 (cold)
Gas:	3 – 4 (preheated)
Baking time:	About 20 minutes
	Cut a lid from each eclair as soon as they come out of the oven (photo 2).
	For the apricot glaze, push
a little apricot jam through a sieve	and heat, stirring continuously. Brush the eclair lids with this mixture.
	For the filling, melt
75 g nut nougat spread	in a small bowl in a water bath over a low heat, stirring continuously. When smooth, leave to cool a little. Beat
250 g (1 pot) double cream	for ½ minute. Sprinkle in
1 pkt cream stiffener	and continue beating until the cream is stiff. Carefully fold in the nougat mixture a spoonful at a time. Spoon the nougat cream into a piping bag (serrated nozzle), and pipe into the eclairs (photo 3). Put a lid on top of each eclair.

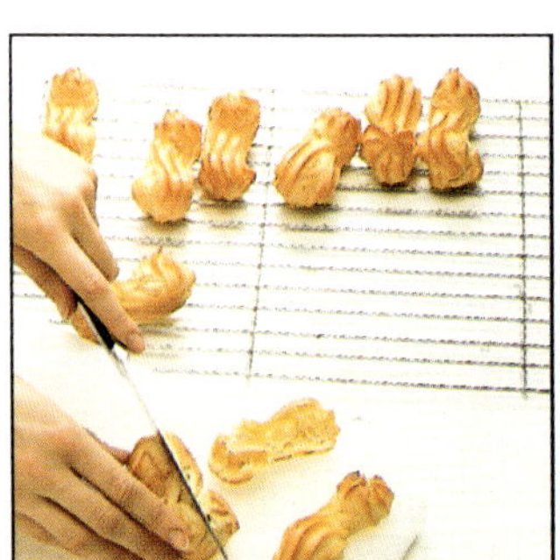

Choux Pastry

Cream puffs
(wholefood cakes)

	For the choux pastry, bring to the boil
125 ml (1/8 l) water	
75 g butter	
sea salt	in a long handled saucepan. Mix together
100 g finely ground wheat	
50 g finely ground buckwheat	Remove saucepan from heat, and add flour all at once. Stir until pastry comes away from the sides of the pan in a smooth ball. Return to the heat for a further minute, stirring continuously. Transfer the hot pastry to a mixing bowl. Using the kneading attachment on the electric mixer, and the highest setting, gradually work in
4-5 eggs	Enough egg has been added when the pastry is very glossy and has a heavy dropping consistency. Work
1 pinch baking powder	into the cold pastry. Use 2 teaspoons or a piping bag to place 20 small heaps of choux mixture on a greased and floured baking sheet. Push into the oven.
Electricity:	
Conventional	200 – 225 (preheated)
Convection	170 – 180 (cold)
Gas:	4 (preheated)
Baking time:	30 – 35 minutes
	Do not open the oven door during the first 15 minutes, as the pastries will collapse. Cut a lid from each cream puff as soon as they come out of the oven. Leave to cool.
	For the filling, soak
3 leaves white gelatine	in
cold water	Wash, drain, cut into halves or quarters
375 – 500 g strawberries	Squeeze excess moisture out of the gelatine. Heat, stirring continuously until dissolved. Mix with
4 tbs maple syrup	Beat
375 – 500 ml (3/8 – 1/2 l) double cream	until almost stiff. Beat in the gelatine mixture. Continue beating until completely stiff. Pipe half the cream into the cream puffs, top with strawberries, pipe the remaining cream on top, and cover lightly with the lids.

Cream puffs

	For the choux pastry, bring to the boil
250 ml (¼ l) water	
50 g butter or margarine	in a long handled saucepan. Mix together
150 g flour	
30 g cornflour	Remove saucepan from heat, and add flour all at once. Stir until pastry comes away from the sides of the pan in a smooth ball. Return to the heat for a further minutes, stirring continuously. Transfer the hot pastry to a mixing bowl. Using the kneading attachment on the electric mixer, and the highest setting, gradually work in
4-6 eggs	Enough egg has been added when the pastry is very glossy and has a heavy dropping consistency. Work
1 pinch baking powder	into the cold pastry. Use 2 teaspoons or a piping bag to place 12 small heaps of choux mixture on a greased and floured baking sheet. Push into the oven.
Electricity:	
Conventional	200 – 225 (preheated)
Convection	170 – 180 (cold)
Gas:	4 – 5 (preheated)
Baking time:	25 – 30 minutes
	Do not open the oven door during the first 15 minutes, as the pastries will collapse. Cut a lid from each cream puff as soon as they come out of the oven. Leave to cool.
	For the filling, wash, trim and stone
500 g sour cherries	Cover with
50 g sugar	and leave to stand to draw juice. Bring to the boil briefly or use
360 g stoned, stewed cherries	Drain the cherries and measure 125 ml (⅛ l) cherry juice (make up with water if necessary). Stir
15 g cornflour	into the juice. Bring to the boil, stir in the cherries, and sweeten with sugar. Beat
500 ml (2 pots) double cream	for ½ minute. Sieve
25 g icing sugar	Mix with
1 pkt vanilla sugar	
2 pkt cream stiffener	Continue beating until completely stiff. Spoon some of the cherry mixture into the cream puffs. Pipe the cream on top, cover lightly with the lids and dust with
icing sugar	

Mixtures suitable for deep frying:

The following cake and pastry mixtures are suitable for deep frying:
- **Choux pastry**
- **Kneaded pastry**
- **Quark and oil pastry**
- **Yeast pastry**

Fat:
It is essential to use the right fat. Neutral tasting, 100 % vegetable fat (e.g. coconut fat) is best. If oil is used, it must never be mixed with solid fat.
Fill the deep fat fryer with enough fat to immerse the pastries. The same fat may be used for a variety of foods (e.g. fish, pastries).
The high temperatures prevent flavours from being transferred. Filter the fat every time it has been used. To do this, pour the fat through a metal sieve lined with kitchen paper.
Fat can be used 6 – 10 times for deep frying.

Temperature:
Fat should be neither to hot or too cold when the pastries are immersed. If fat is too hot, the pastries will brown too quickly, not rise properly, and be underdone inside. If it is too cold, the pastries will absorb too much fat and the fat can start to foam. This foaming can be so strong that delicate pastries can literally be torn apart. As soon as fat starts to foam, its temperature must be raised. Never put too many pastries in the fat at once, and take care when adding new pastries, as this also causes the fat to cool. The temperature of the fat must be checked before each new batch of pastries is fried. The correct temperature is 170 – 190° C. If you do not have a thermometer, you can check the temperature of the fat by holding the handle of a wooden spoon in it. If bubbles form around the wooden spoon, the temperature is right.

Baby doughnuts
(photo p. 232/233)

	Sieve
500 flour	into a mixing bowl with
2 level tsp baking powder	Add
150 g sugar	
½ phial rum flavouring	
3 eggs, salt	
150 g soft margarine or butter	Using the kneading attachment on the mixer, knead the ingredients on a low setting, switching to high. Remove from the mixing bowl and knead on the work surface until you have a smooth ball. If the pastry sticks, refrigerate it for a while. Roll the pastry out to a thickness of 1 cm, and cut out shapes with a small oval pastry cutter. Deep fry in hot
fat	Remove with a slotted spoon and leave to drain and cool. While still hot, dredge with
icing sugar	

Apricot and nut doughnuts
(wholefood pastries)

	Using an electric mixer on highest setting, cream
125 g soft butter or margarine	for about ½ minute. Gradually mix in
100 g pear and date preserve	
grated rind of 1 lemon (untreated)	
sea salt	Keep stirring until the mixture is smooth. Stir in
2 eggs	(½ minute per egg)
200 g low fat quark	Mix together
250 g finely ground wheat	
125 g finely ground buckwheat	
2 heaped tsp baking powder	Stir in on medium mixer setting. Fold in
100 g dried, diced apricots (unsulphurated)	
100 g chopped hazel nuts	Using 2 teaspoons, take pieces of the dough, and deep fry them in hot
fat	until brown all over. Remove with a slotted spoon and leave on a wire rack to drain.

Deep Fried Pastries

Berliner Doughnuts
(photo p. 237)

	Sieve
500 g flour	into a mixing bowl. Add
1 pkt dried yeast	and mix carefully with the flour. Add
30 g sugar	
1 pkt vanilla sugar	
3 drops bitter almond-flavoured baking oil	
1 level tsp salt	
2 eggs	
1 egg yolk	
125 ml (1/8 l) lukewarm milk	
100 g melted, cooled butter or margarine	Mix the ingredients for a moment, using the kneading attachment on the electric mixer and a low setting, then switch to high and knead thoroughly for 5 minutes. If the dough is sticky, add a little extra flour (not too much as the dough should be soft). Cover the dough and leave to rise in a warm place until it is well risen. Remove the risen dough from the bowl and knead it thoroughly on the work surface. Roll out about ½ cm thick, and cut out rounds about 7 cm in diameter with a pastry cutter. Brush the edges of half of the rounds with a little
egg-white	Put a dab of
jam	in the centre of each round. Cover with the remaining rounds, pressing the edges together firmly. Leave in a warm place to rise again. When well risen, deep fry in hot
fat	Remove from the fat with a slotted spoon, allow to drain on a wire rack, and turn in
sugar	

Tip: The Berliner doughnuts can also be brushed with icing. Simply mix icing sugar and lukewarm water until you have a thin paste.

Eberswald piped doughnuts
(photo p. 239)

	For the pastry, bring to the boil
250 ml (¼ l) water	
50 g margarine	in a long handled saucepan. Mix together
150 g flour	
30 g cornflour	Remove saucepan from heat, and add flour all at once. Stir until pastry comes away from the sides of the pan in a smooth ball. Return to the heat for a further minute (photo 1), stirring continuously. Transfer the hot pastry to a mixing bowl. Using the kneading attachment on the electric mixer, and the highest setting, gradually work in
25 g sugar	
1 pkt vanilla sugar	
4–6 eggs	Enough egg has been added when the pastry is very glossy and has a heavy dropping consistency. Work
1 pinch baking powder	into the cold pastry. Spoon the mixture into a piping bag with a large nozzle and pipe rings on to 10x10 cm squares of greased baking parchment (photo 2). Remove the rings from the paper by immersing in hot
fat	and fry until brown on both sides (photo 3). Remove with a slotted spoon and leave to drain on a wire rack.
	For the glaze, sieve
200 g icing sugar	Mix with
2 tbs lemon juice	
2 tbs hot water	stirring until you have a thickish paste. Brush over the doughnuts.

In Germany, Christmas baking would not be complete without lots of honey, syrup, almonds and spices such as cinnamon, cardamom, cloves and nutmeg.
When using honey and syrup, it is important to remember that these ingredients are first melted with sugar, fat and liquid. While it is cooling, the honey (syrup) mixture should be stirred occasionally so that it cools evenly. When hand warm, the mixture is then used with the other ingredients in the recipe.

Marzipanstollen

(photo p. 240/241)

	Soak
250 g raisins	in
4 tsp rum	and leave to stand for a few hours or overnight (if possible). Carefully dissolve
1 pkt dried yeast	
1 tsp sugar	in a bowl containing
150 ml lukewarm milk	Leave to stand for about 15 minutes at room temperature. Sieve
375 g flour	into a mixing bowl. Make a well in the centre. Around the edges of the flour arrange
75 g sugar	
1 pkt vanilla sugar	
salt	
2 pinches cardamom	
2 pinches mace	
1 egg	
150 g very soft margarine or butter	Pour the yeast mixture into the well. Mix the ingredients for a moment, using the kneading attachment on the electric mixer and a low setting, then switch to high and knead thoroughly for 5 minutes. If the dough is sticky, add a little extra flour (not too much as the dough should be soft). Cover the dough and leave to rise in a warm place until it is well risen. Knead again thoroughly on highest setting. Quickly knead in the rum raisins on medium setting with

125 g currants
100 g diced candied lemon peel
100 g peeled, chopped almonds
200 g almond paste

Roll the dough out to a 30x20 cm rectangle. Knead and roll out to a rectangle 30x15 cm. Place this on the dough so that space is left at the long edges. Starting at one of the long edges, roll up the dough fairly tightly and shape into a loaf. Place this on a baking sheet lined with greaseproof paper and leave in a warm place until well risen. Push the baking sheet into the oven.

Electricity:
Conventional: preheat to 250, bake at 150 – 175
Convection: preheat to 200, bake at 150
Gas: 2 – 3 (preheated)
Baking time: 45 – 55 minutes

As soon as the stollen comes out of the oven, brush it with 75 g melted butter and sprinkle with 50 g icing sugar

Meringues
(for using up egg-white)

4 egg-whites
200 g finely granulated sugar

Using an electric mixer on highest setting, beat 4 egg-whites until stiff. Gradually beat in 200 g finely granulated sugar. Spoon the mixture into a piping bag and pipe shapes on to a baking sheet lined with greaseproof paper. Alternatively, use 2 teaspoons to make mounds of meringue mixture on the paper. Meringues should only rise slightly and turn a light cream colour. Push the baking sheet into the oven.

Electricity:
Conventional: 110 – 130 (preheated)
Convection: 100 (preheated)
Gas: 25 minutes on 1, 25 minutes off, 25 minutes on 1
Baking time: 70 – 100 minutes

Cinnamon stars

(for using up egg-white)

	Using an electric mixer on highest setting, beat
3 egg-whites	until stiff. Gradually add
250 g sieved icing sugar	Reserve 2 heaped tbs beaten egg-white. Very carefully (mixer on lowest setting), fold in
1 pkt vanilla sugar 3 drops bitter almond-flavoured baking oil	
1 level tsp ground cinnamon	and half of
275 – 325 g unpeeled ground almonds or hazelnuts	Knead in enough of the remaining ground nuts so that the mixture hardly sticks at all. Roll out ½ cm thick on a work surface sprinkled with
ground almonds or hazel nuts or icing sugar	Cut out stars with a star-shaped pastry cutter and arrange them on a baking sheet lined with greaseproof paper. Brush with the reserved egg-white, which must be of a consistency to brush on smoothly (if necessary add a few drops of water). Push the baking sheet into the oven.
Electricity:	
Conventional	130 – 150 (preheated)
Convection	120 (preheated)
Gas:	1 – 2 (cold)
Baking time:	20 – 30 minutes The biscuits must feel slightly soft when they come out of the oven. Store in cardboard boxes.

Quark Stollen

	Soak
500 g raisins	in
100 ml rum	and leave to stand for a few hours or overnight (if possible). Mix together
500 g flour	
1 pkt baking powder	Sieve into a mixing bowl. Add
150 g sugar	
1 pkt vanilla sugar	
salt	
4 drops bitter almond-flavoured baking oil	
1 pinch ground cloves	
1 pinch ground cardamom	
1 pinch ground ginger	
1 pinch ground nutmeg	
1 pinch ground cinnamon	
a little grated orange peel (untreated)	
2 eggs	
175 g soft butter	
250 g quark	Knead the ingredients with the electric mixer on low, then switch to high and knead thoroughly. Turn out on to the work surface and knead in
250 g peeled, ground almonds	
150 g diced candied lemon peel	
100 g diced candied orange peel	and the raisins. Keep kneading until you have a smooth dough. Shape into a loaf. Push into the oven on a baking sheet lined with greaseproof paper.
Electricity:	
Conventional	preheat to 250, bake at 160 – 180
Convection	preheat to 200, bake at 150
Gas:	2 – 3 (preheated)
Baking time:	50 – 60 minutes
	As soon as the stollen comes out of the oven brush it with
100 g melted butter	and sprinkle with
50 g icing sugar	

Nuremberg "Elisenlebkuchen"

(pastry makes about 40, 6 cm diameter)

	For the pastry, finely dice
75 g candied orange peel or candied lemon peel	and grind
125 g almonds	then, using a mixer on highest setting, beat
2 eggs	until fluffy. Mix together
200 g muscovado sugar	
1 pkt vanilla sugar	Sprinkle in during about 1 minute, and keep beating for a further 2 minutes. Stir in
1 pinch ground cloves	
½ phial rum flavouring	
1 – 2 drops lemon-flavoured baking oil	Mix the almonds with
1 pinch baking powder	and fold into the egg mixture with enough of the candied peel and
75 – 125 g ground hazel nuts*	to make a spreadable mixture. Place 1 teaspoonful of the mixture on each of 40 rice paper circles, and spread (thicker in the centre than at the edges) with a moistened knife. Arrange on a baking sheet and push into the oven.
Electricity:	
Conventional	130 – 150 (preheated)
Convection	120 (preheated)
Gas:	1 – 2 (preheated)
Baking time:	25 – 30 minutes
	For the light coloured glaze, sieve
150 g icing sugar	Mix with
1 – 2 tbs hot water	until it forms a thickish paste.
	For the dark coloured glaze, melt
75 g chocolate	
10 g coconut fat	in a small bowl in a water bath over a low heat, stirring until the mixture is smooth. When the "Lebkuchen" come out of the oven, brush half with the light and half with the dark glaze.

* The amount of ground hazelnuts will depend on the size of the eggs.

Nut crescents
(photo p. 249)

	For the pastry, sieve
300 g flour	into a mixing bowl. Add
100 g sieved icing sugar sugar 1 pkt vanilla sugar salt 1 small egg 100 g ground, slightly toasted hazel nuts	
200 g soft butter	Using the kneading attachment on the mixer, knead the ingredients on a low setting, switching to high (photo 1). Remove from the mixing bowl and knead on the work surface until you have a smooth ball. If the pastry sticks, refrigerate for a while. Roll portions of the pastry into pencil-thick rolls, cut into 6 cm lengths, roll the ends thinner than the middle (photo 2), arrange on a baking sheet lined with greaseproof paper and bake in the oven.
Electricity:	
Conventional	175 – 200 (preheated)
Convection	160 – 170 (preheated)
Gas:	3 – 4 (preheated)
Baking time:	About 12 minutes
	Sprinkle the nut crescents with
icing sugar	as soon as they come out of the oven (photo 3).
Tip:	Confectioner's snow can be used instead of icing sugar.

Syrup and sesame biscuits
(wholefood biscuits)

	Finely grind
250 g wheat	Mix in a bowl with
2 rounded tsp baking powder	Add
250 g syrup, 1 tbs milk	
1 pinch ground cloves	
1 pinch ground mace	
50 g finely diced candied orange peel	
50 g finely diced candied lemon peel	Using the kneading attachment on the mixer, knead the ingredients on a low setting, switching to high. Remove from the mixing bowl and knead on the work surface until you have a smooth ball. If the pastry sticks, refrigerate for a while. Roll out thinly and cut out shapes with pastry cutters. Arrange these on a baking sheet lined with greaseproof paper, and brush with
milk or cream	Sprinkle with
sesame seeds	Push the baking sheet into the oven.
Electricity:	
Conventional	175 – 200 (preheated)
Convection	160 – 170 (preheated)
Gas:	3 – 4 (cold)
Baking time:	About 12 minutes

Lemon hearts
(for using up egg yolks)

	For the pastry, using an electric mixer on highest setting, beat
3 egg yolks	
125 g sugar	
1 pkt vanilla sugar	for 1 minute until fluffy. Beat in
grated peel of 1 lemon (untreated)	
1 pinch baking powder	and enough of
200 – 250 g peeled, ground almonds*	to make a stiff paste. Knead in enough of the ground almonds to make a pastry that hardly sticks. Roll it out about ½ cm thick on a work surface sprinkled with

peeled, ground almonds	
or icing sugar	Cut out hearts with a pastry cutter, arrange on a baking sheet lined with greaseproof paper and push into the oven.
Electricity:	
Conventional	175 – 200 (preheated)
Gas:	3 – 4 (preheated)
Baking time:	About 10 minutes
	For the glaze, sieve
100 g icing sugar	Mix with
1 – 1 ½ tbs lemon juice	to make a thickish paste. Brush over the biscuits when they come out of the oven.
	*The required amount depends on the size of the eggs.

Fruit loaf

	Cut
125 g hazel nuts in half	Dice
125 g dried figs	Sort
250 g raisins	Using an electric mixer on highest setting, beat
3 eggs	until fluffy. Mix together
125 g sugar	
1 pkt vanilla sugar	Sprinkle in during 1 minute, and continue beating for a further 2 minutes. Quickly stir in
½ phial rum flavouring	
1 pinch ground cinnamon	Mix together
125 g flour	
50 g cornflour	
1 level tsp baking powder	and sieve. Set the mixer to low and mix all the ingredients into the eggs with
60 g peeled, chopped almonds	
125 g diced candied lemon peel	Spoon the mixture into a 30x11 cm loaf tin lined with greaseproof paper and push into the oven on the wire shelf.
Electricity:	
Conventional	175 – 200 (preheated)
Convection	150 (cold)
Gas:	2 – 3 (cold)
Baking time:	70 – 90 minutes

Baking for Christmas

Honey cake
(wholefood cake, photo p. 253)

	For the cake mixture, heat
250 g honey	
125 g soft butter	in a pan, stirring continuously. Pour into a mixing bowl, leave to cool. When almost cold beat in
2 eggs	
1 pkt "Lebkuchen" spices	(available in German shops – otherwise mix ground cloves, cinnamon, mace, nutmeg and a little ginger to get a similar flavour)
grated peel of 1 lemon (untreated)	Mix together
375 g finely ground wheat	
1 pkt baking powder	
2 tsp cocoa	and beat in, a spoonful at a time, on medium setting. Add
100 g currants	
100 g hazel nuts	Spread the mixture on a greased baking sheet, and brush with
milk	Sprinkle with
100 g peeled, chopped almonds	and push into the oven
Electricity:	
Conventional	175 (preheated)
Convection	150 (preheated)
Gas:	3 (preheated)
Baking time:	About 20 minutes
	For the apricot glaze, push
5 tbs apricot-peach-maracuja jam	
(prepared with pear juice thickening)	through a sieve, and brush over the cake as soon as it comes out of the oven. Leave to cool.
	For the glaze, melt
200 g plain chocolate	and
a little coconut fat	in a small bowl in a water bath, over a low heat, stirring until the mixture is smooth. Spread over the cold cake. Allow to set. Cut the cake into pieces and store in an airtight tin.

Confectionery

Calvados chocolates
(Wholefood chocolates)
(photo p. 254/255)

	Finely dice
4 dried apple rings	Cover with
3 tbs calvados	and leave to stand for 3 – 4 hours. Finely chop
250 g plain chocolate	Bring to the boil
200 g double cream	Remove from heat, and stir in chocolate and
100 g coconut fat	Stir until melted, allow to cool until semi set, then whisk until creamy. Stir in the pieces of apple and the calvados. Spoon the mixture into a large nozzled piping bag, and pipe blobs into paper cases. Decorate with halved
pistachio nuts	Store the chocolates in an airtight tin in a cool place.

Fruit and nut marzipan loaf
(photo p. 257)

	Knead together
50 g almond paste (sweetened with honey)	
10 g peeled, chopped almonds	
10 g chopped walnuts	
1 tsp sesame seeds	
10 g finely chopped candied orange peel	
1 finely diced prune	
1 finely diced dried apricot	
1 finely diced dried apple ring	Shape the mixture into a loaf. Melt
20 g plain chocolate	and
a little coconut fat	in a small bowl in a water bath over a low heat, stirring until the mixture is smooth. Brush over the marzipan loaf. Leave in the refrigerator until firm. Store wrapped in cellophane paper.

Cinnamon sticks

	Finely chop
200 g milk chocolate	Bring to the boil
100 ml double cream	Remove from the heat and stir in the chocolate,
25 g soft butter	
1 rounded tsp cinnamon	Allow to cool until semi set, then beat until creamy. Spoon into a large nozzled piping bag, and pipe strips 3 cm long on to aluminium foil. Mix together
2 tbs sieved icing sugar	
½ tsp ground cinnamon	Turn the sticks in this mixture, and store in an airtight tin in a cool place.

Nut truffles

	Using an electric mixer, cream
75 g butter	Stir in
75 g sieved icing sugar	
1 pkt vanilla sugar	Break
200 g plain chocolate	into small pieces and melt in a small bowl in a water bath over a low heat. Stir into the butter/sugar mixture. Add ⅔ of
75 g ground hazel nuts (toasted if liked)	Refrigerate the mixture for a while. Shape into small balls, and roll in the remaining hazel nuts. Pack the nut truffles in cellophane bags or sealed glass or china pots, and keep in a cool place.

Fruit balls

(makes about 100)

	Remove stones from
250 g dates	Put through the coarse disc of the meat grinder together with
250 g prunes (stoned)	
250 g dried apricots	Add
grated peel of 1 lemon (untreated)	

2 tbs honey	Mix the ingredients well. With damp hands, shape balls from the mixture. Roll in
80 g ground walnuts or peeled, ground almonds or ground hazelnuts	Leave for a few hours at room temperature. Store the fruit balls in airtight tins.

Truffle delights

	Break
150 g plain chocolate	
100 g milk chocolate	into pieces. Heat together with
200 g double cream	
100 g coconut fat	stirring continuously until the mixture is smooth. Bring to the boil once, then transfer to a bowl. Add
200 g chopped nut nougat bar	Keep stirring until the nougat and chocolate mixtures are well combined. Leave to cool, stirring occasionally. When cool, beat the mixture with an electric mixer until it looks creamy. Spoon small amounts into a piping bag with a serrated nozzle, and pipe into
about 80 paper cases	Decorate with
pistachio nuts	Pack the truffles in aluminium foil or cellophane, and store in a cool place.

Date confectionery
(wholefood confectionery)

	Stone
250 g dates	Cut
100 g almond paste (sweetened with honey)	into as many pieces as you have dates, shape into ovals, and press into the dates to replace the stones. Melt
30 – 40 g plain chocolate	and
a little coconut fat	in a small bowl in a water bath over a low heat, stirring until smooth. Dip the ends of the dates in the chocolate, then refrigerate until set. Store the sweets in airtight tins in a cool place.

Confectionery

Brittle bites

	Heat
20 g butter	
60 g sugar	until lightly browned and the sugar is dissolved. Add
125 g peeled, chopped almonds	Continue to heat, stirring all the time until the brittle has the right shade of brown. Spread on a greased baking sheet. When cold, break the brittle into small pieces. Break
100 g plain chocolate	into small pieces. Mix with
5 tbs double cream	in a small bowl, and melt in a water bath over a low heat, stirring continuously until smooth. Place small heaps of the mixture on aluminium foil, and leave in the refrigerator to set. Pack the brittle bites in cellophane bags or sealed glass or china pots, and store in a cool place.

Fine chocolate crisps
(photo p. 261)

	Break
150 g milk chocolate	
100 g plain chocolate	into small pieces. Melt in a small bowl in a water bath over a low heat with
10 g butter	
1 pkt vanilla sugar	stirring continuously until the mixture is smooth (photo 1). Leave to cool. Stir
75 g desiccated coconut	
½ packet (86 g) cornflakes	into the mixture (photo 2). Put heaps of the mixture into paper cases (photo 3), or place heaps on greaseproof paper. Refrigerate until set. Store in tins or jars in a cool place.

Bread doughs

Sunflower seed rolls

(makes 12 – 14, photo p. 262/263)

	Put
300 g finely ground wheat	
200 g finely ground rye	in a mixing bowl and mix carefully with
1 pkt dried yeast	
1 pkt sourdough extract	Add
1 heaped tsp salt	
375 ml (3/8 l) lukewarm water	Mix the ingredients for a moment, using the kneading attachment on the electric mixer and a low setting, then switch to high and knead thoroughly for 5 minutes. Just before kneading is ended, work in
100 g sunflower seeds (roasted without fat)	leaving 1 tbs for decoration. Cover the dough and leave to rise in a warm place until it is well risen. Remove from the bowl, and knead again thoroughly. Shape into a roll, cut into 12 – 14 pieces and form buns. Place on a greased baking sheet. Leave in a warm place until well risen, then push into the oven.
Electricity:	
Conventional	200 – 225
Convection	170 – 180 (cold)
Gas:	4
Baking time:	About 30 minutes

Country bread

	Put
250 g white flour	
250 g brown flour	into a mixing bowl. Mix thoroughly with
1 pkt dried yeast	
1 tsp sugar, 2 tsp salt	
ground pepper	
4 tbs (60 ml) cooking oil	

250 ml (¼ l) lukewarm water	Mix the ingredients for a moment, using the kneading attachment on the electric mixer and a low setting. Add
125 g sourdough (from the baker)	then switch to high, and knead thoroughly for 5 minutes. Cover the dough, and leave it to rise in a warm place until it is well risen. Remove from the bowl and knead again thoroughly. Shape into a round loaf. Place on a greased baking sheet. Leave in a warm place until well risen. Brush with cold water, make criss-cross cuts about 1 cm deep in the top, and dust with
flour	Push into the oven.
Electricity:	
Conventional	200 (preheated)
Gas:	3 – 4 (preheated)
Baking time:	About 50 minutes

Cheese rolls

	Put
250 g white flour 175 g strong white flour	into a mixing bowl. Mix thoroughly with
1 pkt dried yeast 1 tsp sugar, 1 tsp salt ground pepper 250 ml (¼ l) lukewarm water	Mix the ingredients for a moment, using the kneading attachment on the electric mixer and a low setting, then switch to high and knead thoroughly for 5 minutes. Towards the end of the kneading time, knead in
150 g coarsely grated cheese	Cover the dough and leave to rise in a warm place until doubled in size. Remove from the bowl and knead again thoroughly. Shape into about 10 oval rolls. Place these on a greased baking sheet. Leave in a warm place until well risen. Beat
1 egg yolk 1 tbs water	Brush over the rolls. Sprinkle with
50 g coarsely grated cheese	Push into the oven.
Electricity:	
Conventional	175 – 200 (preheated)
Convection	160 – 170 (cold)
Gas:	3 – 4 (preheated)
Baking time:	About 25 minutes

Almond loaf

(photo p. 267)

	Put
500 g flour	into a mixing bowl. Mix thoroughly with
1 pkt dried yeast 75 g sugar 1 pkt vanilla sugar ½ tsp salt, 1 egg 250 g (1 pot) lukewarm double cream 100 g melted, cooled butter	Mix the ingredients for a moment, using the kneading attachment on the electric mixer and a low setting, then switch to high and knead thoroughly for 5 minutes. If the dough sticks, add a little flour (not too much as the dough should be soft). Cover the dough, and leave it to rise in a warm place until well risen. Remove from the bowl and knead again thoroughly, quickly kneading in
150 g raisins 100 g unpeeled, sliced almonds (photo 1)	on medium setting (photo 2). Put the dough into a greased loaf tin (35x11 cm). Leave in a warm place until well risen. Brush with water. Push into the oven.
Electricity:	
Conventional	175 – 200 (preheated)
Convection	160 – 170 (cold)
Gas:	3 – 4 (cold)
Baking time:	About 40 minutes As soon as the loaf comes out of the oven, brush it with water (photo 3).

Marzipan plaits
(photo p. 269)

	Put
500 g flour	into a mixing bowl. Mix thoroughly with
1 pkt dried yeast	
1 heaped tsp salt,	
1 tbs cooking oil	
125 ml (1/8 l) lukewarm milk	
250 ml (1/4 l) lukewarm water	Mix the ingredients for a moment, using the kneading attachment on the electric mixer and a low setting, then switch to high and knead thoroughly for 5 minutes until you have a smooth dough. Cover the dough, and leave it to rise in a warm place until well risen. Remove from the bowl and knead again thoroughly. Shape into a roll and cut this into 12 pieces. Remove 1/3 of each piece of dough, and roll until 15 cm in length. Roll the larger pieces of dough to 30 cm in length. Lay the large pieces of dough in a horseshoe shape on the work surface with 1 short roll between each. Make plaits from two long and one short piece until all the pieces are used up. Press the ends down firmly or fold back under the plait. Place the plaits on a greased baking sheet. Leave in a warm place until well risen. Brush with water and sprinkle with
poppyseeds	Push into the oven.
Electricity:	
Conventional	200 – 225 (preheated)
Convection	170 – 180 (preheated)
Gas:	4 (preheated)
Baking time:	25 – 30 minutes
	Place a bowl of hot water on the bottom of the oven while the plaits are baking.

Alphabetical Index of chapters

G

H

I

K

L

M

N

O

P